THE HEBREW
PHYSIOLOGUS

First edition of the Tsemaḥ Tsaddik

THE HEBREW
PHYSIOLOGUS

ANIMALS AND CREATURES IN THE *TSEMAḤ TSADDIK* OF LEON MODENA

VERED TOHAR

UNIVERSITY OF WALES PRESS
2025

© Vered Tohar, 2025

All rights reserved. No part of this book may be reproduced in any material form (including photocopying or storing it in any medium by electronic means and whether or not transiently or incidentally to some other use of this publication) without the written permission of the copyright owner. Applications for the copyright owner's written permission to reproduce any part of this publication should be addressed to the University of Wales Press, University Registry, King Edward VII Avenue, Cardiff CF10 3NS.

www.uwp.co.uk

British Library CIP Data

A catalogue record for this book is available from the British Library
ISBN   978-1-83772-243-3
eISBN   978-1-83772-244-0

The right of Vered Tohar to be identified as author of this work has been asserted in accordance with sections 77 and 79 of the Copyright, Designs and Patents Act 1988.

Designed and typeset by Chris Bell, cbdesign
Printed and bound by CPI Group (UK) Ltd, Croydon, CR0 4YY

For any General Product Safety Regulation (GPSR) enquiries, please contact: Logos Europe, 9 rue Nicolas Poussin, 17000, La Rochelle, France   contact@logoseurope.eu

SERIES EDITORS' PREFACE

THE UNIVERSITY OF WALES PRESS series on Medieval Animals explores the historical and cultural impact of animals in this formative period, with the aim of developing new insights, analysing cultural, social and theological tensions and revealing their remarkable resonances with our contemporary world. The series investigates ideas about animals from the fifth century to the sixteenth, and from all over the world. Medieval thought on animals preserved and incorporated a rich classical and mythological inheritance, and some attitudes towards animals that we might consider as having characterized the Middle Ages persisted up to the Enlightenment era – and even to the present day.

Series Editors: Diane Heath and Victoria Blud

CONTENTS

Acknowledgements	xi
Introduction	1
The World of the Pre-Modern Jewish Storyteller	1
Some Background on *Musar* Literature	4
Tsemaḥ Tsaddik as a Hebrew *Physiologus*	12
Tsemaḥ Tsaddik as a Translated Adaptation of *Fiore di Virtù* (*'Flower of Virtue'*)	16
Tsemaḥ Tsaddik as a Hebrew *Florilegium*	23
The Art of Leon Modena's Storytelling	25
The Flexibility of a Bold Author: Original Contents in *Tsemaḥ Tsaddik*	29
Between Cultural Systems: *Tsemaḥ Tsaddik* as a Cultural Crossroads	33
The Creatures in this Anthology	36
Notes	38
Works cited	44
The Text	49
1 On the virtue of love, in general	49
2 On the love of God	52

viii | The Hebrew *Physiologus*

3	On the love of father, mother and relatives	54
4	On friendship	55
5	On natural love	58
6	On the love of women	59
7	On envy	61
8	On happiness	63
9	On worry	65
10	On peace	68
11	On anger	70
12	On charitable acts	73
13	On cruelty	76
14	On generosity	78
15	On greed	81
16	On admonition	84
17	On flattery	88
18	On diligence	90
19	On foolishness	93
20	On justice and judgement	95
21	On wrongdoing and lawlessness	98
22	On loyalty	100
23	On dishonesty and deceit	102
24	On truthfulness	104
25	On lying	106
26	On bravery	108
27	On cowardice	110
28	On largesse	112

29	On vanity	113
30	On strength and fortitude	115
31	On fickleness	117
32	On temperance	119
33	On lasciviousness	122
34	On humility	123
35	On pride	125
36	On abstinence	127
37	On drunkenness and gluttony	129
38	On modesty	131
39	On adultery	133
40	On integrity and good manners	136

Index	143

ACKNOWLEDGEMENTS

THIS BOOK was conceptualised thanks to Dr Diane Heath, from Canterbury Christ Church University, whom I met at a Reinardus Conference. She was the one who saw the potential of the text I presented there and who encouraged me to move forward with this project. My heartfelt thanks also go to Sarah Lewis, from the University of Wales Press, for her professionalism and patient guidance, without which this book would never have been published..

I also wish to thank Mrs Ethelea Katzenell from the bottom of my heart for translating my text and some of the rabbinical references, as well as the poetic Hebrew text itself. She also edited the book intelligently and with dedication.

I greatly appreciate being granted access to the Rare Books Collection of Bar-Ilan University, along with the kind help of its manager, Mr David Ben-Naim, and being given permission to use certain illustrations scanned from the New York 1875 edition.

Last, but not least, many thanks to the Akaviyahu Fund of Bar-Ilan University for its generous support towards the publication of this book.

INTRODUCTION

THE WORLD OF THE PRE-MODERN JEWISH STORYTELLER

TRY TO IMAGINE a Jewish reader in 1600, one who knows how to read Hebrew, his sacred tongue, just as he knows how to read Italian and perhaps several other languages as well. This reader is most likely a religious family man and relatively well off, who can afford to buy books to read at his leisure, and he is always looking for decent books that he can bring into his home, present to his guests, and read them to his wife and children.

Imagine that man entering a printer's shop that sells Hebrew books in Venice, Verona, Prague or Amsterdam. The bookseller offers to sell him a new Hebrew book by Leon of Modena, a rabbi and preacher, renowned in Venice. As the potential reader browses through the book, he discovers that it is indeed printed in the sacred Hebrew language and consists of short chapters. Beside the beautiful Hebrew calligraphy, he sees breathtaking illustrations. Indeed, this is not a cheap book but, according to the chapter titles, it deals with human virtues and vices, and is meant to teach good manners. Will he buy the book? Would you have bought it if you had been in his position?

This monograph deals with one of the most spectacular Hebrew works of the pre-modern age, first published in 1600 in Venice by Daniel Zaniti and later in additional printed editions.

2 | The Hebrew *Physiologus*

The significance of this work stems from the fact that it had been influenced by classical Latin literature, medieval Christian ethics literature, and the classic Jewish works. Modena's work includes descriptions of human virtues and vices by presenting examples of such behaviours among living creatures found in a series of folktales. Leon of Modena's work is enigmatically titled *Tsemah Tsaddik*, which means literally 'pious plant' but was called *Fiore di Virtù* ('*Flower of Virtue*') in its Italian rendition, although, for this English rendition, I prefer the double entendre title *Righteous Growth*.

Yehudah Aryeh Modena was born in Venice, Italy, in 1571 and died there in 1648. Apparently, he was an avid lover of tales, which he would collect and insert into his writings. We know that he was also a popular storyteller, who did not just embed these tales in his books, but he told them as part of his famous public sermons, given before large audiences. Many ideas for such stories he took from the Jewish biblical and rabbinic sources.[1] However, since he was also attentive to the world of European folktales, which had numerous, intricate ties to Hebrew literature, traces of many non-Jewish tales also found their way into Modena's works.[2]

Indeed, *Tsemah Tsaddik* stands at the hub of the present discussion, albeit intending officially to deal with moral matters but, between the lines and beyond all the statements, it is rife with the love of tales, whatever their origins. This daring work, written originally in clear Hebrew, integrated dozens of tales, which together form a marvellous and unique ensemble of characters and voices, from near and far, East and West. *Tsemah Tsaddikk* was initially meant to be the Hebrew translation of a popular Italian book on practical ethics and of an ancient Latin book called the *Physiologus*. Modena was an especially brave and creative translator, who sometimes made so many changes while translating (to make it suitable for the Jewish readership) that almost all traces of the original text became obscured.

Modena's noteworthy love for folktales, no doubt, played a significant part in their impact on the world of the Hebrew tale. Modena's sensitivity to the narrative mode rewarded Jewish culture

Introduction | **3**

with dozens of new tales – his resultant adaptations, making their first appearances in Hebrew writings. These old, recycled tales, in their new Hebrew renditions, were destined, from his day on, to become part of the corpus of Hebrew literature.

As such, this book presents the readership with this modestly sized pre-modern work, after being apprised of its disproportionate significance, and Modena's emphasis on creatures and what might be learnt from them. This book was written to take advantage of the then-novel printing technology, so that it might reach as many readers as possible; in other words, it was a pre-modern economic project, attesting to a combination of economic and cultural forethought and planning. If only for the large quantity of illustrations, clearly, beyond its contents, a sizable investment was also made in its design. It was meant for the Hebrew reader, who could enjoy its clear and beautiful language. Modena's book played an important role towards the incorporation of new narrative themes into the corpus of Hebrew tales. Some of the contents of his book are bold, despite having been written by a respected authority figure in the Jewish community, in the sacred tongue, and within a conservative, religious society – much like the rest of pre-modern European society. In fact, this book served both as an exemplar of the concept and a template for the format of ethical prose containing embedded folktales and fables, including descriptions of living creatures.

This study asks the following questions: How can a text be designed to flow easily between diverse literary formats and genres – such as rabbinic (religio-legal) literature; Jewish ethics literature (henceforth, *Musar* literature) and folk literature – and still manage to fulfil all its predetermined goals? How might ethical instruction be made available and appealing to the readers, so they might improve their values, by means of compelling tales, without losing sight of the didactic morals of those stories and recognising the connections to the best European literature and philosophy of that period, all the while without arousing the antagonism of the orthodox readers?

4 | The Hebrew *Physiologus*

SOME BACKGROUND ON *MUSAR* LITERATURE

The term 'M*usar* literature' is a general name incorporating a wide range of literary formats, each one has its own system of poetic conventions (e.g., sayings, proverbs, exempla, fables, legends) – all meant to improve the characters of the readers, to help them become better Jews. Usually, M*usar* literature focuses on vices and virtues of human beings, often highlighting the punishments (of those who do not mend their ways) and the rewards (for the observant and righteous) both in this life and in the afterlife.[3] During the hundreds of years between the tenth and eighteenth centuries, M*usar* literature served as a central arena for the creation of Hebrew prose, alongside Jewish law, biblical commentary, historic chronicles and mysticism. Jewish M*usar* literature is characterised by the relatively brief development of each idea under discussion, and by its simplicity of expression and purposefulness. This type of literature seeks to provide practical interpretations of the Jewish codes for behaviour, to implement abstract theological ideas, and to promote religious and ethical values for the broadest Jewish readership.[4] M*usar* literature is not just a unique branch of educational Jewish ethics, it is also a special branch of popular Jewish literature.

This book studies Modena's case that illuminates a key cultural phenomenon in which literature is serving ethics; or more precisely, international folk literature is used in the service of Jewish moral education. Modena's work integrates ethics and poetics. This bond was never necessary. In principle, ethics and poetics are two distinct branches of philosophy. Ethics deals with human nature and behaviour, while poetics deals with the various forms of human expression. Ethics asks, what is 'good'? How can one attain 'goodness'? Poetics asks, what distinguishes a certain literary work from all the rest of human creativity?

Aristotle devoted two of his essays, one to ethics and another to poetics.[5] Since Modena lived in an Aristotelian world, they both shared the same basic assumptions, it is easy to begin clarifying

Passerine.
From *chapter* 12, '*On charitable acts*'.

Modena's concepts accordingly. Aristotelian ethics poses the question: who is a 'good' person? To which Aristotle replies, the 'good man' is one who has positive attributes ('virtues'). As such, Aristotle claims that we must ask: how can a human being personally acquire virtues? Aristotle places human personality and behaviour into a dichotomous world of good and evil, drawing a straight line from an individual's personality to his actions. This means that virtues are prerequisites for good deeds, and good deeds lead people to lives of satisfaction and happiness. During the Middle Ages, with the development of the Jewish concept of an afterlife, in addition to having a temporal good life, one might strive to also attain eternal life in Heaven, as promised to those who are 'good'.

Aristotelian poetics poses the question: what is a 'good' creation? This relates to the three forms of drama: tragedy, comedy and epic poetry. Aristotle established clear rules for the writing of each of these dramatic forms, so that they would draw an audience and achieve the best results – the experience of catharsis.

6 | The Hebrew *Physiologus*

By reading his *Poetics* (*c*.335 BCE), one can understand that an artistic work is, first and foremost, an expression of collective values; therefore, the role of the poet is to create the best expression of those values. The categorical rules that Aristotle proposed suggest a strict and well-formulated conceptual framework, within which the poet functions.

Thus, according to Aristotle, once an artistic work has expressed the collective values, and produced a cathartic experience, reconfirming said values, by means of some heroic figure, art is both motivated by the collective ethics and motivates awareness of those collective ethics. In other words, Aristotle believes that there is a strong connection between ethics and poetics, since ethics is expressed via poetics, whereas poetics is the individual actualisation of ethical principles. And, if so, art is integrally bound to reality, primarily since art expresses the actual terrestrial values of the Earth's consumers.

Musar literature, more than any other type of Jewish literature, is the clarion of the values of the world's consumers – as per the definition of its function in the world of phenomena. The pre-modern Jewish authors of *Musar* literature intended to transform their readers into better people as an outcome of their reading, it meant to alter their personalities, thus having a beneficial effect on their behaviours. *Musar* literature was assigned a transformative role, as a tool that gathers the individual readers into one group, sharing similar behaviours; for example, to encourage the readers to give charity, or to promote their respect for their parents. When a *Musar* book includes not only prose sermons, but also *Musar* tales, those embedded tales also take on the responsibility for encouraging the readers to become ethically aware – hopefully leading to improvements in their personalities and subsequent behaviours. As such, these tales embedded in a *Musar* book take on the poetic burden, having ethical consequences, as well. Thus, *Tsemah Tsaddik*, studied here, is defined as being a *Musar* book that includes *Musar* tales. It is a text that intentionally inserts tales for the readers' ethical instruction, allegedly serving as collective behavioural anchors. The *Musar* tales found in *Tsemaḥ Tsaddik* seem to provide support for the prose *Musar* texts in which they are embedded, such that the narrative prose and the non-narrative prose portions form an ensemble of different voices together, sharing one clear and consistent ethical orientation.

Note, however, that the Hebrew language is a gendered language, and its learned sages were overwhelmingly men. As such, the use of 'he' or 'him' or 'a man' in ethicosocial discussions generally encompasses either 'all Jews' or 'all humans', unless the discussion is about a specific male personage. Also, God is frequently addressed using capitalised masculine forms.

Fate determined that the moralistic content of *Tsemaḥ Tsaddik* would stand in stark contrast to Modena's actual biography – he was a complicated man, at odds with himself and his surroundings, whose genius was revealed in his youth, but who suffered tribulations and calamities as an adult. It seems that all the good characteristics discussed in his book were denied to him; on the contrary, he apparently had all the vices.[6] Nonetheless, it is hard not to be sympathetic and understanding about his faults and weaknesses, in light of the marvellous works that he left in his wake, the most outstanding of which was *Tsemaḥ Tsaddik*, a literary pearl of wisdom.

Modena wrote many essays in Hebrew and Italian, the majority of which were published during his lifetime, the rest posthumously. His masterpiece, *Tsemaḥ Tsaddik*, was published when he was only twenty-nine years old, a father with many children, and renowned amid Italian Jewry for his sermons and public speaking. His income was partially derived from the publication of his books, yet, for various reasons (such as many mouths to feed), he found himself in economic distress throughout most of his life. According to his own testimony in his autobiography – considered the first Hebrew autobiography ever published – he was addicted to popular gambling dice games, involved in bad financial investments, and was regularly pursued by creditors. He derived little pleasure from his children and his marriage.

8 | The Hebrew *Physiologus*

Modena's many writings teach us that he was both an intellectual and aware of his own faults, with a broad education and openness to his non-Jewish surroundings, despite his personal hardships. Moreover, his works describe the daily life of Jews in Italy, in general, and in the Venetian ghetto, in particular. His interest in contemporary scientific research methods was born of his fascination with the amalgamation of different traditions and cultural influences. As such, and not merely due to his personal history, Modena was an outstanding author in the field of Hebrew literature, who left a rich legacy in his wake.

Regarding his life story and family history, Modena wrote about them openly in an unpublished essay found after his death. That manuscript was handled by his grandson after his death in 1648. In it, Yehudah Aryeh de Modena unfolded his entire history, in clear language and a naturalistic style, especially his personal hardships: miserable marriages; rebellious and sinful sons and their brides; his compulsive gambling; and his conflicts with creditors and loan sharks. Besides this, his testimony also offers a unique peek at the lives of the Jews in the Venetian ghetto, in his day, and provides a great deal of information on the Printers' Republic at that time – a book of interest not only to literary scholars, but also to historians and those researching medieval culture.

It is obvious that Modena did an excellent job finding suitable materials when compiling *Tsemah Tsaddik*. Its language is, for the most part, clear and intelligible, even to twenty-first-century readers. The contents flow well, and the tales are captivating. It is no wonder that this book is still popular 425 years later. It would not be an exaggeration to say that Modena was a consummate storyteller, a man rife with tales from many periods and cultures, who then introduced them to his readers. Perhaps his many years as a preacher in his community also trained him to relate to these tales as effective tools for fashioning public opinion and inculcating certain ideas. However, occasionally, some of his tales undermined themselves, suggesting covert meanings contrary to the overt message that he intended to present, as will be demonstrated in examples below. Nevertheless, even the conflicting messages raised further interest in this book. As is the case in all good stories, even Modena's embedded *Musar* tales had lives of their own, existing in distinction from the initially planned didactic aspect. Anyone who delves deeply into this work will read about the depths of the human soul, on its wishes, its desires, its deviations and weaknesses.

The entirety of the tales found in *Tsemaḥ Tsaddik*, by virtue of their inclusion in the *Musar* literature genre, create a symbolic road map for their readers' behaviours; however, they do not replace the Musar texts, nor do they claim to do so. Practically speaking, they are non-essential – some say excessive – in any *Musar* discussion. And yet, many of these tales are born of ancient *mythos* ('the myths'), in which *logos* ('logic') is opposite to *nomos* ('the law') and frequently steals the show. It is difficult for the myths to co-exist simultaneously with the law. Modena knew this, but his attraction to the mythical, to the irrational, motivated him to attempt a combination of the two – a decision that he knew would have a positive impact on those who read *Tsemaḥ Tsaddik*.

The tales that appear in *Tsemaḥ Tsaddik* are very different from the usual, accepted repertoire of Hebrew tales, even in Modena's day. Many of them were new and strange to the Jewish reader, some were adaptations of Christian parables from the New Testament, altered to suit the Hebrew reader, or they were adaptations of ancient Greco-Roman literary texts and classical mythology. Had Modena wanted merely to publish a collection of folktales in Hebrew, one that was easy to read and more potable, he would have chosen the usual ones that were already more commonly known. From the narrative contents found in *Tsemaḥ Tsaddik*, we can discern that Modena wanted to set a literary precedent, as well as one in the *Musar* literature. He wanted to leave his mark on the field of Hebrew literature, to refresh old fables, to present new plots. Modena was a storyteller *par excellence*, with a novel agenda; and he was certainly not a conservative messenger relaying the usual messages.

10 | The Hebrew *Physiologus*

It seems that the 'Angel of History' assigned Modena a much more important task than he had planned for himself. Indeed, there is no doubt about his declared intentions, according to which he had planned to write books about Jewish virtues, debates on religion, faith, Jewish law, Jewish life and collected sermons on the Hebrew Bible (*Torah*). Yet, at the same time, Modena was also a cultural activist. *Tsemaḥ Tsaddik* is an example of Modena's talent for telling stories – probably by heart, orally and not just in writing – since he was known a popular and experienced preacher. Although no evidence remains of his oral sermons, his published writings give us the opportunity to read his words today and to be impressed by the extent of his knowledge and the richness of his education. There is also no doubt that Modena's personal bookshelves were extensive and replete with a diverse wealth of books.

By genre, *Tsemaḥ Tsaddik* is a *Musar* book. Its morality is deeply rooted in Jewish culture, although it is an abstract idea. To demonstrate this moral code, its values must first be made visible. Jewish values are organised in a conceptual hierarchy of good and bad, what behaviour is more desirable and what is less desirable. These values are an integral part of everyday life, not distinct from it. A moral lifestyle is expressed by means of concrete actions, thoughts about those deeds, in ongoing, autonomous reflection, as a person constantly and consciously studies and evaluates his or her own behaviour, out of an awareness that he or she can always do better. Indeed, Michael Lambek asserts, as conscious, social human beings who use language, we are fundamentally ethical creatures.[7] The paradox lodged within this situation is that the very nature of ethical thought includes both being judgemental and creating a behavioural hierarchy, while by its nature, language is not neutral and already contains certain biases. People tend to judge not only themselves but also others. In other words, value judgements occur within social frameworks, so that they are also causes of confrontations, sanctions, legislation and formal or informal punishment.[8]

Introduction | 11

In fact, *Tsemaḥ Tsaddik* belongs to a relatively distinct subset of ethics literature, that of books on 'virtue ethics.' The Jewish *Musar* books, like the medieval Islamic and Christian ethics literature, consisted of a series of chapters, each one dedicated to a different virtue that the reader should adopt or strengthen, or to various vices that the reader was advised to weaken. Many of these books on human attributes, not only the Jewish ones, discussed virtues, such as patience, loyalty and generosity, and also vices such as cruelty, dishonesty and cowardice. The goal of these works was to promote personal and conscious change in the readers, that would make their lives happier and more fulfilling in this world and in the afterlife. Modena was well aware of the social role he was taking upon himself by writing such a book, as suggested by the book's title, cover and introduction.

The cover title is based on the biblical verse (Jeremiah 23: 5): 'See, a time is coming – declares the Lord – when I will raise up a righteous branch of David's line. He shall reign as king and shall prosper, and he shall do what is just and right in the Land' – entirely future orientated, as a consoling prophecy, suggesting to the readers that they may also have a future of integrity and justice. In regard to the book's goal, Modena defines this in his Introduction: 'to assess [a person] in accordance with his attributes, recounting them from start to finish, be they good or bad – [to determine] what each person can do to fix them and to acquire divine favour'. That is to say, the book presents both the virtues and the vices to those who want to mend their ways by self-improvement. Afterwards, Modena adds an additional goal: 'I have named it *Tsemaḥ Tsaddik*, so it might also join the ranks of the books that promote right-eousness to the masses.' Here, Modena plays with the phonetic similarity between the Hebrew noun *tsaddik* ('a righteous man') and the verb *matsdik* ('justifying'), thus emphasising his justified role as a public servant to his readership – that by writing this book, he is rewarding his audience with his good intentions.

In addition, this book's title refers to the world of floral imagery, as did other *Musar* works, such as *Tomer Devorah* ('*Deborah's*

12 | The Hebrew *Physiologus*

Palm Tree') and *'Arugot ha-Bosem* (*'The Fragrant Flower-Beds'*). Another group of philosophical, Kabbalistic and *Musar* works found its inspiration in metaphors about 'the path', such as *Orḥot Tsaddikim* (*'The Ways of the Righteous'*); *Sefer ha-Yashar* (*'Book of the Straight Path'*); *Moreh Nevukhim* (*'Guide for the Perplexed'*); and *Ma'alot ha-Middot* (*'The Degrees of the Virtues'*). Yet another group is distinguished by the use of the 'light' metaphor, for example, the *Zohar* (*'Brilliance'*) and *Menorat ha-Ma'or* (*'Shining Candelabra'*). Thus, *Tsemaḥ Tsaddik* is certainly situated within the accepted conventions, although one cannot ignore the fact that the floral metaphor is anchored to the Christian tradition (discussed further below).

TSEMAḤ TSADDIK AS A HEBREW *PHYSIOLOGUS*

Tsemaḥ Tsaddik, indeed, integrates several distinct and diverse areas. It is a hybrid of the Renaissance *florilegium* and medieval parables, integrating Jewish *Musar*, Islamic ethics and Christian ethical literature. It also combines vegetative symbolism with images from the world of animal fables. Most of all, this work attests to Modena's involvement in the Christian world around him, with which he was well acquainted.

Following the format of the original Italian text, there are no fewer than thirty-five different species of creatures mentioned in *Tsemaḥ Tsaddik*. Some are mythological (the Siren, Basilisk, Caladrius, Phoenix and Unicorn), one was real but is now extinct (the wild bull, Aurochs), and the others are quite real (e.g., bear, raven, toad, ant, etc.). In the time of the Renaissance, due to the absence of Hebrew names for those creatures not mentioned in the Hebrew Bible, Modena identifies them by their foreign nomenclature, as in these cases: the *Castor*, known in modern Hebrew as *boneh* ('beaver'); the *Rospo*, now called *karpadah* ('toad') in Hebrew; and the *Pirnitso*, called *ḥoglah* ('partridge') in Israel. Modena also distinguished between three different species of predatory bird; known in modern Hebrew as *nesher* ('eagle'), *baz* ('falcon') and *peres* ('vulture'). However, in two tales, one about a virtue and the other

Sirens.
From chapter 17, 'On flattery'.

about a vice (representing contrary attributes and behaviours), he used the same term *falconi* to describe some generic bird of prey, for lack of specific Hebrew names for each of the two species.

Modena makes parallel associations between certain creatures' behaviours and certain human attributes (virtues and vices), usually in the classic, conventional manner, as found in *Aesop's Fables* (*c*.600 BCE) and in the Hebrew Bible; for example, the ant as a symbol of industriousness, the fox representing cunning, and the lion as a sign of bravery.[9] Yet, although *Aesop's Fables* showed meticulousness by mentioning only real creatures, Modena allowed himself the liberty of flights of imagination, even attributing human traits to mythological creatures and creating novel and surprising associations between the wild ass and 'abstinence', the honeybee and 'justice', the sparrow and 'fickleness', and the dove and 'modesty'.

The matter of this connection between living creatures and the literature of virtue ethics is worthy of further attention. Similar works did not exist in Hebrew virtue ethics literature, nor even

14 | The Hebrew *Physiologus*

in the corresponding Arabic literature. Modena's work was highly innovative at that time.

The chapters of *Tsemah Tsaddik* express the correspondence between the worlds of the lesser living creatures and of Humanity, since the main attributes being discussed in these chapters characterise both creatures and human beings. Each value described by Modena, he relates to some living or mythical creature, and the accompanying illustrations, for most of these values, also have generic images of the relevant creatures, as customarily presented in *Aesop's Fables*. For certain attributes, Modena makes original assignments of specific creatures to the virtue or vice that they represent, despite the fact, for example, that there is no clear zoological connection between bats and 'adultery', nor between moles and 'lying'.

The connection between living creatures and human beings was made in medieval literature in two distinct types of literature – the Aesopian and the Bestiary. Aesopian literature, in the very popular spirit of *Aesop's Fables*, consists of collected parables, also adopted into Hebrew literature. Works such as the *Fox Fables* by R. (i.e., Rabbi) Berechiah ha-Naqdan (translated in the thirteenth century), *Fables from the Distant Past* by Isaac b. (i.e., *ben*; 'son of') Solomon Ibn Sahula (written in 1281) and *Kalīlah wa-Dimnah* ('*Kalilah and Dimnah*') (translated into Hebrew during the twelfth century), are, among others, the most famous and beloved parable collections in Hebrew. They enjoyed wide distribution, thanks to their combined provision of education and amusement. The term 'Aesopian' was also attached to other collections of parables, indicating the ancient source from which they all drew their material – *Aesop's Fables*.

Bestiary literature was less familiar in Hebrew literature; a form of medieval, didactic literature, serving as a sort of descriptive lexicon of living creatures, 'beasts', having a certain affinity with human behaviour, part of the general field of religious tales, ultimately intended to instruct the reader on how to behave and what to think.[10]

Introduction | 15

The archetypal representative of non-Jewish European (soon to be termed 'bestiary') culture was the anonymous Greek work from the second century CE, titled *Physiologus* ('*Naturalist*'),[11] apparently written in Alexandria and translated into Latin in the fourth century. This work served as the basis for the later medieval formats, focusing on creatures, to transmit didactic messages to humans. Also worth noting are Isidore of Seville's *Etymologiae* ('*Etymologies*'),[12] particularly Book 12, in Latin, dedicated to living creatures, and *Le Bestiaire Divin* by Guillaume (William), Cleric of Normandy.[13]

The *Physiologus* contains an amalgamation of early scientific texts and narrative prose. Its structure consists of brief chapters, each chapter devoted to a different creature, plant or inanimate object in Nature, including mythical and legendary creatures. Each one is described by all its characteristics, after which, based on the description, an allegorical interpretation of the creature's attributes is equated with a human attribute, good or bad. Sometimes, this description is accompanied by biblical stories from the Hebrew Bible or the New Testament.[14] These tales were particularly focused on the Genesis stories about Creation and the Garden of Eden, as well as on spectacular descriptions of significant creatures throughout the Hebrew Bible, such as the whale that swallowed Jonah, and the lion that Samson overcame. Unlike *Aesop's Fables*, which tended to be orientated towards social messages, reflecting its pagan, agricultural society, the *Physiologus* was orientated towards Christian religious interpretations (discussed below).

The *Physiologus* is a work consisting of fifty-one chapters that provide allegorical descriptions of human characteristics as expressed by a long line of living creatures, plants and special stones. It was structured such that each fundamental element in Nature got its own chapter, and most also have a descriptive woodcut print alongside.[15] Unlike *Tsemah Tsaddik* or other similar anthologies, the *Physiologus* does not tell tales, although it does hint at many of those found in the Hebrew Bible, the New Testament and

16 | The Hebrew *Physiologus*

the Apocrypha, such as: 'The three men in the fiery furnace' (Daniel 3: 8–29); 'Susanna and the elders', based on a deuterocanonical text (Daniel, Chapter 13); 'Judith and Holofernes', based on the deuterocanonical Book of Judith; and 'The story of Queen Esther', based on the Scroll of Esther, etc. The *Physiologus* even mentions the destruction of the First Jerusalem Temple by Babylonian King Nebuchadnezzar (II Kings 25: 8–9; Jer. 52: 12–3). Here, we are focusing on the resemblance between the world of the creatures, the visible world, and the invisible world of Christian concepts.

The *Physiologus* is attempting to create sort of a science of the soul, based on the assumption that human beings and living creatures belong to the same biological system in Nature. In its rhetoric, it does not assess the value of the attribute under discussion, but rather presents the natural world to the reader by means of the parallel between the creatures and human believers or sinners, and the connection between those behaviours and characteristics and those of Jesus or the Devil, or other theological concepts. The orientation of this work is specifically religious and replete with quotes from the Hebrew Bible and the New Testament, in support of its claims.

The central idea that may be gleaned from the *Physiologus* is that it has no essential interest in the creatures themselves, beyond their symbolic interface with humanity; it is Humanity, not the creatures, at the heart of this work.

TSEMAH TSADDIK AS A TRANSLATED ADAPTATION OF *FIORE DI VIRTÙ*

In the introduction to Modena's Hebrew text, *Tsemah Tsaddik* ('Righteous Growth'), he explicitly writes that his is not an original book, at least not in the formal sense; however, Modena does not name the work that had served as his primary template and inspiration, other than the fact that it was written in Italian. In the nineteenth century, Jewish scholar Moses (Moritz) Steinschneider first identified the work: *Fiore di Virtù* ('*Flower of Virtue*'), which Steinschneider called

Introduction | 17

Flower of the Virtues (lit., 'Flower of the Good Values'), as being the basis for Modena's *Tsemaḥ Tsaddik*. Steinschneider also noted the early twelfth-century Latin work *Disciplina Clericalis* ('*Training of the Clergy*') by *converso* Petrus Alphonsi (née, Moses Sephardi), as a potential source of ideas. The resemblance between the earlier Italian and the later Hebrew texts became the subject of a brief article, almost a footnote in his research.[16] Later, in the twentieth century, Emanuel Bin-Gorion also identified the connection with *Fiore di Virtù*, but he posited that the spirit of *Tsemaḥ Tsaddik* was closer to that of an anonymous medieval Latin work from the late thirteenth century, titled *Gesta Romanorum* ('*Deeds of the Romans*').[17]

Actually, Steinschneider was correct in his identification. The Italian ethics book *Fiore di Virtù* was written long before Modena's period, apparently in the thirteenth century, by Tommaso Gozzadini, and it was a commonly found manuscript across Europe, so popular that it had even been translated into various local European vernaculars.[18] With the advent of the printing press, this book was printed in Italian and other languages, including German, Spanish, Romanian and Russian. It was equally popular in print and was successfully reprinted again and again throughout Europe. Modena had become acquainted with this very popular Italian ethics book and decided to translate it into Hebrew.

Apparently, Modena was captivated by the contents of the Italian bestseller, by the tales it contains and by its fascinating illustrations. Constantly engaged in seeking materials to publish to generate income, he thought that by means of a Hebrew translation, with certain adjustments to suit his Jewish readership, he might achieve financial success. So, that was what he did. The end product before us is purportedly a translation of that Italian book, but completely revised to fit the Jewish ethos. It was meant to yield economic profits, as had the popular original. Modena, like many other authors, wanted his book to be a bestseller, so he settled on a format that he felt would both suit his Hebrew readers and also suited the ancient tradition of Jewish *Musar* literature and virtue ethics.

18 | The Hebrew *Physiologus*

Modena may also have thought that his translation project was expanding the Hebrew readers' knowledge, exposing them to great classics from ancient times, in the spirit of the Renaissance, by establishing common denominators between the contemporary Jewish and popular Italian cultures.

Modena did not hide the fact of his translation, acknowledging it in his Introduction, which is evidence of his and his readers' openness to the Christian world, their thirst for new content, and their curiosity regarding the world around them. Both the author and his readership were firmly ensconced in the quintessential Renaissance experience, much like the Venetian nobility, that was fashioning its world according to Greco-Roman influences alongside the secular Renaissance culture.[19]

In any case, the question arises: why translate an Italian work into Hebrew that all the Jews in Italy could read in the original Italian? And why translate it into the sacred Hebrew tongue, rather than into a secular Judeo-Italian vernacular? Indeed, in Modena's day, there were already several *Musar* virtue ethics books in Yiddish that enjoyed a wide distribution and satisfied the leisure-time needs of their readers who could not read Hebrew. It seems that part of Modena's strategy was to ensure that this book could be distributed not only to the Italian-Jewish community, but to Jews the whole world over, all across Europe and even in North Africa and Asia. His choice to use the Hebrew language created the potential for a much broader readership, despite the uncertainty regarding the actual number of Hebrew-reading Jews in the world at the end of the Renaissance period. From the outset, this choice granted *Tsemah Tsaddik* special standing, of which Modena was, no doubt, aware. An additional assumption about the reason for translating a popular Italian work into Hebrew arises from the internal hierarchy of the literary systems. Hebrew readers had a very high regard for translated literature, which supposedly served as an intercultural bridge to European cultures. Educated readers considered translated literature as having a very high status, even higher than that of the original works, such that the translators of European literature into Hebrew considered themselves to be prestigious messengers, who would bring their readers the current artistic pinnacles, the spirit of the times, as it were, into their own Jewish culture. Modena's strategy was to create a common language with the culture of the majority, which Italian Jews considered a necessity. Thus, *Tsemah Tsaddik* became a part of the chain of transmission originating from *Fiore di Virtù*, which, surprisingly, gained the book a solid position in Hebrew literature, as well as spawning later translations of Modena's Hebrew rendition into a plethora of European languages.

Nevertheless, he was unwilling to translate all the tales found in the original *Fiore di Virtù* and he omitted a number them. The following are those folktales that Modena decided were unsuitable for inclusion in his Hebrew work, intended for the Jewish readership.[20] This group of rejected tales included many that originated in the Hebrew Bible, but, as may be seen, their plots were often very different, warping the original versions and deviating from the divine biblical messages. The following are brief summaries of the excluded tales.

'Cain and Abel' (Chapter 8, 'Jealousy')

Cain saw that his brother Abel was prospering, his possessions were increasing, and that these boons were received from God. Out of jealousy, he clubbed his brother to death. Cain and Abel were the first brothers in the world, and that was the first case of bloodshed in the world.[21]

The legate' (Chapter 9, 'Happiness')

There was a legate (a high-ranking Roman officer) who had an abundant love of God. So much so, that he sailed across the Mediterranean Sea to get to the Church of the Holy Sepulchre (in the Holy Land). When he arrived there, he cried for joy and died of happiness and devotion. Those who accompanied him called for physicians, but they pronounced him dead. When they performed a post-mortem, above his heart was written,

20 | The Hebrew *Physiologus*

'My sweet love, Jesus'. Then, the physicians determined that he had died of happiness and claimed that a joyful death is much quicker than a sorrowful one.

'Uriah's letter' (Chapter 12, 'Anger')

King David fell in love with Bathsheba, Uriah's wife. David slept with her, and she became pregnant by him. David ordered Uriah, who was stationed with the army, besieging a city, to go home and lay with her, so that the newborn might be thought to be his. However, Uriah refused to go anywhere near his wife. David became furious and sent Uriah to deliver a letter to his commander. The letter instructed that they go to battle and that Uriah should be placed in the most dangerous position on the front line. When the battle began, the soldiers near Uriah ran away, leaving him alone, and he was killed.[22]

'The ten plagues' (Chapter 17: 'Regret')

God warned the Egyptian Pharoah via Moses, several times, to release His people from bondage. But the Pharoah's heart was hard. So, God sent the Pharoah ten plagues, so he would change his mind: 1) it rained blood; 2) it rained frogs; 3) there were swarms of flies; 4) beetles covered the ground; 5) a botanical disease killed all the plants; 6) another disease killed all the animals; 7) there were swarms of crickets; 8) all the first born died; 9) a thick fog turned day into night; and finally, 10) the Pharoah and his military men drowned in the Red Sea.[23]

'Lot and his daughters' (Chapter 22: 'Deceit')

God sent two angels to the depraved city of Sodom, where unnatural acts were being committed. A man named Lot, who was one of God's pious believers, received those angels in his home. They informed Lot that he must vacate his land, because they are about to destroy the city. Lot took his wife and two daughters and left. Once they were outside the city, Lot's daughters decided to deceive him so that they might lay with him. So, they got him drunk until he did not recognise them. Lot laid with his eldest daughter and then also with the younger one. Thus, both his daughters sinned with father and became pregnant by him.[24]

'Gloria and Ammon' (Chapter 26: 'Falsehood')

A young woman named Gloria, who was the daughter of Caesar Anastasius, fell in love with one of the Caesar's men, named Ammon. He, however, abstained from getting involved with her, out of fear of the Caesar. Gloria, who was angry at Ammon, decided to take revenge on him. One day, when he walked past her room, she began to scream and tell everyone that he had tried to rape her. Ammon was caught and brought before the Caesar, but he denied the charge. Gloria was also brought before the Caesar and questioned, but she did not answer. One of the Caesar's men said in jest, 'Maybe she's lost her tongue?' It turned out that her tongue had, indeed, vanished, as a punishment for her lying. The Caesar witnessed the miracle and freed Ammon, and Gloria's tongue returned, in proof of the truth. Thanks to this miracle, Gloria entered a monastery to serve God for the rest of her life.

'The death of Samson' (Chapter 27: 'Bravery')

Samson was the strongest man in the world and had achieved great things. His strength came from his natural long hair (Judges 16: 16). The Philistines, against whom he fought, sent a woman named Delilah to deceive Samson and cut his hair. When Delilah had done this, they caught Samson and blinded him. One day, they took him to their temple, where masses of people had gathered to verbally abuse him. Samson asked a young lad to lead him to the central pillar, supporting the structure. Then, Samson whispered to that youth: 'Quickly, run outside! Once you are outside the temple, blow your horn so I'll hear you.' The lad did so, and when Samson heard the horn, he hugged the pillar and pulled it – and the whole temple came tumbling down. Samson shouted, 'Let Samson die with his enemies!' Thus, Samson and everyone who was there perished.[25]

22 | The Hebrew *Physiologus*

'The robber and the monk' (Chapter 32: 'Indecision')

A robber went to confess to a monk, and when the monk told him that he should try to repent for his sins by fasting and praying, the robber replied that he did not know how to pray and was unable to fast. So, the monk said to him, 'If so, you must bend your knee before every cross you see from now on'. The robber accepted his punishment and promised to fulfil the monk's command, and the monk forgave all his sins. When the robber left the monk, his enemies arrived and he began to flee from them. And, suddenly, he saw a cross before him and remembered his pledge. The robber knelt immediately before the cross – and his enemies killed him on the spot. Then, the monk saw an angel come down and carry the soul of the robber to the Garden of Eden, and he was filled with emotions of anger and heresy: how could a man who had sinned all his life go to Heaven with so much respect for such a tiny deed? So, the monk decided to leave the monastery, to live a hedonistic life of pleasures. On his way there, the Devil took control of him, and he fell off a cliff and died. His soul was taken to Hell because he had been inconsistent.

'The fall of the angels' (Chapter 36: 'Pride')

God created the most beautiful and noble angel in the Garden of Eden, but that angel became so proud that his heart desired to oppose God. When God saw this, he sent His archangel, Michael, to banish the proud angel from the Garden, along with all his followers. Thus, pride joined all the other sins.[26]

'Adam and Eve' (Chapter 38: 'Covetousness')

When God created Adam and Eve, He placed them in the Garden of Eden and allowed them to do whatever they wished. He forbade them only to eat the fruit of the tree standing in the centre of the Garden. When God left them there, the Devil came to Eve and tempted her to eat the apple. When Eve realised that she had sinned, she decided to find a partner in sin, and succeeded in convincing Adam to eat the apple as well. Due to this sin, we have all been sentenced to death. As such, God's first negative commandment was against covetousness, considered one of the greatest sins in the world.[27]

'The creation of the world' (Chapter 41: 'Moderation')
First, God created the Garden of Eden and the land, then He organised all the rest of the things. He separated day from night, and everything that came between the morning and the evening became one day. On the second day, He separated the heavens from the waters, and so land was created. On the third day, He gathered all the water in the ocean and commanded that the land yield plants of all kinds. On the fourth day, He created the Sun to shine by day and the Moon and stars to shine by night. On the fifth day, He created all manner of animals and birds. On the sixth day, He fashioned Adam from clay in His image, after which He created Eve from a rib He took from Adam's chest when he was deep asleep. Then, God told them, 'Be fertile and multiply and fill the Earth. Dominate the birds and the heavens, the fishes and the sea, and all the creatures upon the land'. On the seventh day, He rested from His work.[28]

All these tales were replaced by our sages' rabbinic tales, found in Jewish sources. The legends, 'Isaiah's death'; 'Ulla in Babylonia'; 'The deaths of the two sons of R. Tavut'; 'Elijah and the stinky man'; and 'R. Joshua and the young boy and young girl' replaced non-Jewish, foreign tales that Modena did not wish to translate, so he chose these from the rabbinic literature.

TSEMAḤ TSADDIK AS A HEBREW FLORILEGIUM

The genre of the *florilegium* grew out of an educational system developed during the Renaissance, in which textual studies were predicated on the selection of the most significant quotations.[29] The basic premise of this system was that, by copying wise quotations, the students would absorb the best ones, which would continue to blossom in their consciousness. Written in

24 | The Hebrew *Physiologus*

the introduction to a German book in the *florilegium* genre, was: 'A book is like a garden you can put into your pocket.' The choice of the world of 'flora' as the basis for one's connection to the world of knowledge was well rooted in the Middle Ages, when illustrators of manuscripts typically drew flowers framing texts and as calligraphic decorations above certain of the authors' and translators' script letters.[30] In late antiquity, when codices replaced scrolls, a 'page' was termed '*folio*', meaning 'leaf', as it is to this day, even in Hebrew, '*aleh*, means both a leaf and the page of a book. Thus, 'leafing' through a book is like plucking leaves from a tree. Naturally, this metaphor is rooted in the Book of Genesis, since it was the fruit of the forbidden 'Tree of Knowledge' that enabled humankind to distinguish between right and wrong.[31]

The *florilegium* (pl., *florilegia*) is an anthology of quotes taken from the writings of experts in a certain field, primarily the writings of the Church Fathers and of Greek and Roman philosophers about its central topic. The literal meaning of this Latin term is 'a gathering of flowers'. Today, such a work is termed an 'anthology' or 'collection'. The *florilegium* is a collection of sayings by thinkers, meant to disseminate knowledge; thus, its distinction.[32] The Latin term *florilegium* appears in the Greek as '*anthología*' and has a few parallel terms in Hebrew, such as: the medieval word *yalkut* ('satchel'); the Renaissance term *ma'aseyf* ('gathering') of Haskalah ('Jewish Enlightenment') literature; and on to *mivhar* ('selection'); *leket* ('pickings'); *mikra'ah* ('reader'); and *osef* ('collection') in modern Hebrew.

The use of the metaphor of 'picking flowers', as representative of creating a collection of knowledge, spread during the Renaissance period and was and has remained widespread in didactic literature to this very day.[33] This genre was created in parallel with the printing revolution and contributed to the wide distribution of books, granting more access to the reading audience. Even the cover illustration of the 1487 Venetian edition of *Fiore di Virtù* showed a monk standing between two pairs of trees in an open field, picking a flower from a tree. In the 1490 edition, the monk is standing between two pairs of trees in the courtyard

Introduction | **25**

of the monastery; and in the 1491 Florentine edition, even Jesus and angels had been added. In those cases, the monk represented 'everyman', suggesting that the reader should behave like the monk.[34] The changes in these illustrations indicate the dialectical tension between moral, humanistic education and doctrinal Christianity, at least regarding these questions: What is the source of the truth? What is the hierarchy between Humanity and God? It seems that the 1491 edition wanted to create a synthesis between the two.

THE ART OF LEON MODENA'S STORYTELLING

One of the unique characteristics of *Tsemah Tsaddik* that distinguishes it from other virtue ethics books found in Jewish culture and in general, is the relative profusion of complete tales included in the body of the work, comprising most of the text. Contrary to the common conventions in literature on values – in which the primary text is composed of morality sermons with a few, individual tales interspersed here and there, or not at all – the internal proportions in *Tsemah Tsaddik* are reversed.

There are no fewer than forty tales in Modena's forty chapters. Each one deals with a virtue or vice found in human beings, human nature or behaviour, which the author either praises or condemns, as a representative of Jewish society. The number forty, marking the number of chapters, was already considered a typologically significant number in the Hebrew Bible, one that connects some highly significant Jewish historical events: forty days of the Flood (Genesis 7: 17); forty years that the Children of Israel wandered in the desert (Num. 14: 33); forty days and nights that Moses spent on Mount Sinai (Deut. 9: 25); forty years of peace and quiet in the Land of Israel in the time of the judges (Judg. 3: 11); and more. In the rabbinic sources, the number forty symbolises repentance (i.e., the return to faith) and God's forgiveness: forty days of repentance between the first day of the Hebrew month of Elul and the Day of Atonement; the age forty is considered the age of wisdom: 'At forty, wisdom' (tractate *Avot* 5: 21);

Unicorn.
From chapter 33, 'On lasciviousness'.

forty days of divine match-making: 'forty days before an embryo is formed a Divine Voice issues forth and says: The daughter of so-and-so is destined to marry so-and-so' (tractate Sotah 2a: 9); R. 'Akiva began studying Torah (the Hebrew Bible) at the late age of forty: 'What were the origins of Rabbi 'Akiva? They say that he was forty years old and had still not learned anything' (Avot d'Rabbi Natan 6: 2); and R. Hillel emigrated from Babylonia to the Land of Israel aged forty: 'Hillel the Elder went up from Babylonia at the age of forty, attended the Sages for forty years, and led Israel for forty years' (Sifrei Devarim 357: 33). As such, Modena's decision to have forty chapters representing forty attributes was laden with significance.

Modena brought forty tales to make forty chapters, listed here by their titles, in order: 1) On the virtue of love, in general; 2) On the love of God; 3) On the love of father, mother and relatives; 4) On friendship; 5) On natural love; 6) On the love of women; 7) On envy; 8) On happiness; 9) On worry; 10) On peace; 11) On anger; 12) On charitable acts; 13) On cruelty; 14) On generosity;

15) On greed; 16) On admonition; 17) On flattery; 18) On diligence; 19) On foolishness; 20) On justice and judgement; 21) On wrongdoing and lawlessness; 22) On loyalty; 23) On dishonesty and deceit; 24) On truthfulness; 25) On lying; 26) On bravery; 27) On cowardice; 28) On largesse; 29) On vanity; 30) On strength and fortitude; 31) On fickleness; 32) On temperance; 33) On lasciviousness; 34) On humility; 35) On pride; 36) On abstinence; 37) On drunkenness and gluttony; 38) On modesty; 39) On adultery; and 40) On integrity and good manners.

This list gives us an idea of what was required of a Jew to become a better person, at least in Modena's eyes, and one may compare this list to those found in Christian virtue ethics. Thus, for example, the vice of 'sloth' or 'laziness', one of the seven deadly sins in Christianity (punishable by damnation), is not found among the vices discussed in *Tsemaḥ Tsaddik*, nor does 'despair' appear. Moreover, two key virtues that are highly characteristic of Jewish thought – 'charitable acts' and 'love of family' – are both absent from the Italian *Fiore di Virtù*.

Each one of these topics is presented in detail, with arguments and illustrations, in a brief chapter with a similar format. Each begins with a prosaic discussion on the specific topic, supported by relevant biblical verses and rabbinic sayings. Afterwards, in most of the chapters, creatures that exhibit the relevant attributes are mentioned, and an explanation is given regarding the connection between that creature and the attribute being studied. The theoretical discussion concludes with relevant sayings by well-known philosophers, usually followed by one tale or sometimes two, which relate to the chapter's topic. Each chapter is also accompanied by a woodcut print, illustrating the subject matter.

The genres of these tales vary: rabbinic tales; biographical legends; theodical legends; historical legends; martyrological legends; expanded biblical stories; animal parables; exempla; and myths. This variety attests to the attempt to create as colourful a collection as possible of fascinating narrative fables, rather than restricting the contents and formats to the usual and expected.

28 | The Hebrew *Physiologus*

In line with the different genres, the repertoire and the characters are also diverse: mythical heroes and literary characters (Medea, Damocles); historic figures (Alexander of Macedon, Aristotle, Priam, Lykourgos); biblical figures (King David, Elijah the Prophet, Isaiah the Prophet); rabbinic authorities (R. 'Akiva, Naḥum Ish Gamzu, Dama b. Netina); and archetypical figures (the king, the philosopher, a miser, a military captain). This varied list also shows Modena's tendency to expand the repertoire of each reader's knowledge by spreading this panorama of characters and situations.

Nevertheless, not all the tales are perfect matches for the subject of the chapter in which they are embedded; some have scant connections or are barely relevant. For instance, in his Chapter 18, dedicated to the virtue of 'diligence', Modena placed a tale, the moral lesson of which is that people should not put off acting on their decisions.[35] While in Chapter 20, there is a tale about the justification and acceptance of divine judgement, on 'justice and judgement', despite there being no direct connection between the two subjects.[36] Bear in mind that that Modena recorded some tales from memory – thanks to his expertise and rhetorical skill (as also expressed in his public sermons and before his students) – or perhaps certain original texts were simply unavailable.[37] It is also quite likely that the version in Modena's possession had already been paraphrased from the original by someone else; he may also have read some of them in Italian, and his book presented his original translation. Modena exhibited great flexibility during this project, essentially allowing himself a free hand to rewrite the folktales that had enticed him to create his outstanding collection in the field of Hebrew literature.

In his book *Rhetoric* (fourth century BCE), Aristotle associated human emotions with the power of 'rhetorical persuasion', that is, that basic human emotions influence moral decisions.[38] Thus, tales brought to support some logical claim, might themselves become tools that activate emotionality. The dramatic qualities with which narrative plots are imbued might transform a tale into a primary means of persuasion, so that a tale might overwhelm a logical argument. Following Aristotle's reasoning, we can understand why these tales are situated at the beginning and end of discussions on morality; Aristotle had already claimed that they are the most important parts of the text. According to him, the unconventional use of words – as in metaphors – seems to elevate the contents. In other words, the tactic of inflating the language draws attention of the readership to the words being used and their meanings; as such, a tale about 'flattery' may arouse – unfortunately or happily – more attention than straight Musar talk about it. Thus, although tales on 'flattery' are considered conceptually marginal, since they do not contribute theoretical contents to the discussion, they are, however, most important for the rhetoric, by helping to strengthen the emotionalism of the reading. This also explains why many books on ethics, including Jewish Musar books, find it difficult to resist the incorporation of tales in those texts, although they are unnecessary on the ideational level. In this regard, descriptions of creatures relevant to the contents of the text's discussion, serving as opening tales, bring the theoretical discussion topic closer to the reader, by reintroducing him or her to it by means of familiar artistic conventions.

THE FLEXIBILITY OF A BOLD AUTHOR:
ORIGINAL CONTENTS IN *TSEMAH TSADDIK*

More than half of the volume of Tsemah Tsaddik consists of original contents. This does not refer only to Modena's original texts, since I have already described the masterfully constructed patchwork quilt created by cited quotations interspersed amid the Musar texts. Modena's originality is also expressed, in this case, by his familiarity with numerous canonical Jewish texts from where he was able to pluck those materials suitable for integration into a pedagogical patchwork quilt of his own unique design.

Anything that Modena felt was inappropriate for his Jewish readership was either deleted or blurred. Thus, for instance, Modena chose not to translate the Italian chapters on 'jealousy'

30 | The Hebrew *Physiologus*

and 'happiness' and skipped over the New Testament quotations and the words of the Church Fathers, replacing them with sayings by the Jewish Sages, taken mostly from the *Babylonian Talmud*. Similarly, certain woodcut prints, which had appeared in the Italian Florentine edition of 1491, were not used in *Tsemaḥ Tsaddik*, because they picture intimate relations between men and women. Also omitted were woodcuts found in the 1487 Venetian edition, illustrating concepts from Christian folktales and thought. The Hebrew rendition contains mainly woodcuts of living creatures, and some were added by Modena, in lieu of those he had censored.[39]

Chapter 3 in *Tsemaḥ Tsaddik* deals with familial love; the love of father, mother and relatives. There was no chapter like this in *Fiore di Virtù*, it therefore comprises entirely Jewish sources and, apparently, is completely in accordance with Modena's personal perceptions and reflects this value – without which a Jewish ethics book is incomplete. This chapter is especially interesting because it reflects the manner in which Modena himself views this subject matter, as well as attesting to Modena's extensive knowledge of the contents of the Jewish sources. However, we also learn that he may have been unfamiliar with the original sources of foreign philosophic writings, since he did not even bother to format this chapter like the others and he did not search for this topic in western philosophy; rather, he drew on his own knowledge of the Hebrew Bible and rabbinic literature, using only the Jewish sources throughout Chapter 3.

A quintessential example of how Modena rewrote the Italian original may be seen in his treatment of Chapter 32 in *Fiore di Virtù*, 'Inconstancy'. In the Italian source, there was an embedded tale, 'The robber and the monk' (see full plot above), attributed to a Christian book titled *Vite dei santi Padri* (*'The Lives of the Holy Fathers'*), written in 1330.[40] In the Italian version, there is a closing line that reads: '[Therefore, Jesus said] Not he who begins, but he who continues all the days of his life, he will be saved.' This was meant to demonstrate the vice of 'inconstancy' (parallel to Chapter 31 'On fickleness' in *Tsemaḥ Tsaddik*). This story was omitted

Introduction | **31**

from *Tsemah Tsaddik*, due to its Christian nature and values, which were completely foreign to Judaism, just as he omitted Jesus' quotation, the epilogue, the Christian moral of that story, which Modena replaced with the Talmudic legend: 'King David's failure' (tractate *Sanhedrin* 107a: 2).

In this context, Modena's choice is very interesting, since the Hebrew narrative tradition in the *Hagighah* and *Sanhedrin* tractates, Rashi's commentary on tractate *Sanhedrin*, and other versions have a deeply rooted Jewish folktale greatly resembling the original version of the Christian rendition of 'The robber and the monk'. This Jewish version is titled 'The pious man and the tax collector' and talks about two people who died on the same day – one who had been pious and observed the biblical commandments all his life, and the other who was a wicked tax collector. Yet, the funeral of the pious man was despicable and sparsely attended, while that of the tax collector was large and respectable. A friend of the deceased pious man began to wonder about God's justice and had a vision in which he saw his pious friend enjoying heavenly pleasures, while the tax collector was tortured in Hell. In his vision, this friend received an explanation that his pious friend had sinned once in all his days, while the tax collector had only obeyed one *mitsvah* ('Jewish commandment') in his lifetime – and both their funerals were meant as repentance for that lone sin and as reward for that lone *mitsvah* – but actually, each one, based on their lifelong behaviours, had gone where they deserved to go in the afterlife. The friend was relieved and admitted that his complaints against God were mistaken.

Indeed, this Jewish folktale, 'The pious man and the tax collector', brings up the debate about human deeds in this life, and reward or punishment in the afterlife. Unlike the Christian approach, the Jewish story presents the ethos of unbroken faith and the tallying of a lifetime's worth of observance (doing *mitsvot*) and commission of sins. As in this case, Modena's choices of narratives are both interesting and challenging, no less than his manoeuvring between familiar tales and those less appropriate for use.

32 | The Hebrew *Physiologus*

An additional and interesting example of the dialectic between change and conservatism, as dealt with by Modena, is found in the folktale titled 'The strange deeds of the Angel'. In this case, as in the previous folktale, a familiar, traditional Jewish version also exists, attributed to Elijah the Prophet and titled 'Elijah's strange deeds'. In this instance, Modena preferred a direct translation from the Christian text, suggesting that he may not have been familiar with the Jewish version. There are great differences between Modena's version and the accepted Jewish one.[41]

All told, about one-third of the tales in *Tsemah Tsaddik* come from the rabbinic literature – the Talmud, the classic *Midrash* (homiletic, non-legal rabbinic works) and later *Midrash*. This attests, contrary to Modena's own declaration, that he had translated an existing book – in fact, most of the original tales were replaced or altered significantly to suit the Jewish, Hebrew-reading audience. The replacement of certain original folktales with others changed the weight of the non-Jewish stories in the book, highlighting the great effort made by Modena to prevent conflict amid the readership. Likewise, it is a testament to Modena's virtuosity, his expertise regarding the sources, and his ability to fish out a suitable, relevant substitute tale from the source pool.[42]

As for Modena's success, members of his generation could not attest to it, but there is authentic witness testimony from a reader in the nineteenth century – Jacob Druckerman, editor of the 1899 New York edition of *Tsemah Tsaddik*, wrote in his introduction to the book that he admits that what drew his attention and that of other readers of his generation were the tales, because people pressured him into publishing this new edition:

> I'm not exaggerating when I say that nothing in Hebrew literature had smelled so sweet, because *Tsemah Tsaddik* was different than the other books, that speak directly about Jewish values. I'll shamelessly admit that I have frequently tried to read *Musar* and virtue ethics books, but I was only able to read two or three pages before retreating, unable to finish what I had started.

Introduction | **33**

But it was totally opposite with this book – I began to read a few pages and couldn't put it down, until I finished the entire book, because drew me in with its words of wisdom and wonderful parables in each and every chapter, especially the stories about the nature of living creatures, historical events, and the words of philosophers. This book had a mighty and huge impact also on other people who read it and learned a great deal, and it was they who emboldened me to publish it for the third time, for the benefit of the public.[43]

BETWEEN CULTURAL SYSTEMS: *TSEMAH TSADDIK* AS A CULTURAL CROSSROADS

Tsemah Tsaddik symbolises the attempt to create a bridge between the Jewish reader at the end of the Renaissance – located in the margins of society – and the dominant arena of the Christian literary world. It highlights the connection between cultural systems, reflecting Modena's openness to and awareness of the world around him, and displaying his ability to make the right associations, thus enabling the adoption of certain foreign materials, by fitting them to suit the lives of his readership.

This literary enterprise enabled Modena to create novel literary texts within the Jewish literary corpus, without losing contact with the Christian texts. Modena was trying to be a citizen of the world in his status as an author; seeking to draw from both worlds and to remain in both. Nonetheless, in reality, Modena was present and absent in each of those two systems, since the Christian perspective considered him a Jewish author, while the Jewish world considered him an Italian translator. The essence of this point is critical for an understanding of his status as an author in the dominant society and for comprehending the problems of his status as an author trying to belong to several literary systems at once.

From the external perspective of minorities, observing the parallel dominant society from both sides is not entirely negative. This double perspective led Modena to make, for himself and for

34 | The Hebrew *Physiologus*

his readers, sporadic revisions in the Jewish social and personal ethos to mirror the Christian ethos. Therefore, each omission that Modena made from the Italian text signified his disagreement with or inability to accept the original. Every tale he added to his Hebrew version from the Jewish bookshelf, expressed an alternative scale of values. Essentially, *Tsemah Tsaddik* expresses a quiet clash of cultures, a war reflecting the deep cultural conflict with which all the Jews in the Diaspora had to cope by the end of the Renaissance.

Tsemah Tsaddik was created in the world of the printing press and was written by a man who was well-versed in the ways of the printing industry. Modena was fully aware of the power of the press, and he went about as one confirming the claim that a person can make a living by making books. It is possible to learn about the reception and impact of the *Physiologus* from the wealth of copies made over the years, even after it had spawned other literary formats, as well as its many popular translations into all European languages.

This might have been an idealised construction of a man whose Bible study has become his art, and who wishes to share his treasures with his community or even with every Jewish Hebrew reader. In practice, however, Modena barely made a living and never really earned enough due to personal difficulties, coping with his addictions, his family problems and dealing with the Venetian underworld.

Accordingly, any additional rewriting of a work is fixed in the broader cultural context in which it is located. Albeit *Tsemah Tsaddik* is a didactic collection, but that is not its only strength. With the addition of the striking illustrations and the sizable volume of its contents dedicated to the tales, following the decision to translate an Italian bestseller, clearly Modena was trying to produce a cultural product that would be widely welcomed and that would bring its author economic prosperity relative to his period. Thus, *Tsemah Tsaddik* also served as an exemplar of a product for cultural consumption, typical in the age of printing, in which the economic aspect of the book's production was a significant factor in author/reader relations. The plentitude of manuscript copies made of

Tsemaḥ Tsaddik, from the same edition printed in Venice, attest to the excellent reception of the work, and that it was much in demand – although we have no idea how much payment authors received in their lifetimes.

The issue of the reception of this book is fascinating, considering its contents. Modena's statements that it was translated from an Italian-Christian source, contains sayings by Church Fathers and classical philosophers, and includes pagan myths and legends – and, moreover, the book's many, sometimes provocative illustrations – did not put off the community of Hebrew readers. Modena's edition is a product of the interaction between the Jewish and Christian worlds and attests to the thirst for new content and the existence of intellectual curiosity about the surrounding world. Both the author and his readers were ensconced in a definitively Renaissance present, a sort of relationship bubble, in which these Venetian nobility and Greco-Roman culture had become amalgamated, forming the Renaissance culture.[44]

A possible explanation for this phenomenon begins with the fact that, at the start of the seventeenth century, subject matter taken from the Greco-Roman myths was not considered threatening by Jewish readers. It may be assumed that the contemporary Christian culture and its myths faced by the Jews were much more threatening than the remnants of any ancient pagan culture. As such, entrepreneur editor Modena, in the spirit of the Renaissance, rediscovered ancient world treasures out of intellectual curiosity and artistic appreciation.

Tsemaḥ Tsaddik exemplifies how universal Jewish material may be revealed anew. This Jewish *Musar* book spans the gaps between the particular and the universal, paving an important new cultural path, one with its own specific value. Not all the values that Modena presented are necessarily Jewish ones; indeed, that is how this work demonstrates a uniting, rather than divisive, ethos.

Modena was a man living in a multilingual space and his writings were meant for a community of readers that also existed in a multilingual environment. It then follows that whenever

36 | The Hebrew *Physiologus*

he wrote a Hebrew work, he also had to contend with the fact that it was not a vernacular and had only a partial vocabulary, which he had occasionally to supplement with words from Italian or French. Alongside his Hebrew works, he also wrote essays in Italian, meant for his non-Hebrew reading audience. Modena's successful handling of the multilingual reality was a testament to his flexibility, a trait required of all who wished to survive in that environment. Again, *Tsemaḥ Tsaddik* serves as an unmistakably clear example of such multiculturalism; thus, this book resembles a sort of time capsule, storing the Jewish Diaspora experience within (as per the example below). It also made *Tsemaḥ Tsaddik* a representative of the multilingual aspect of pre-modern Hebrew literature. Moreover, the great variety of literary types and topics characteristic of *Tsemaḥ Tsaddik* make it a rarity.

THE CREATURES IN THIS ANTHOLOGY

As in the original Italian, Modena's Hebrew version, *Tsemaḥ Tsaddik*, mentions thirty-five different creatures. In this instance, Modena changed nothing. *Tsemaḥ Tsaddik* follows precisely the list of creatures and the attributes that they represent, parallel to *Fiore di Virtù*. These creatures form a very important axis in this work because they connect the theoretical conceptualisations from the words and works of philosophers and biblical verses with stories that represent specific individual events. The discussions on the attributes of these creatures are essentially passages, intermediary links, between the theoretical ethical values and the specific human behaviours. The necessity for the symbolism that each creature represents, even at the start of the seventeenth century, shows us how much creatures have always played a significant part in human thought within each historical context.

Yet, this is not merely a cognitive matter. Placing creatures at the centre of discussions, as the heroes of their situations, is a literary phenomenon already suggested in biblical Hebrew texts such as (Genesis 3: 1), 'Now the serpent was the shrewdest of

Introduction | 37

Raven.
From chapter 9, 'On worry'.

all the wild beasts', and as a metaphor in Proverbs (6: 6): 'Lazybones, go to the ant!'[45] However, animal parables became a more dominant form in the early rabbinic period, termed 'rabbinic literature', and most had their parallels in *Aesop's Fables*.[46] Clearly, in the Middle Ages, with the translation of important anthologies into Hebrew, these creatures became integral parts of the literary menu of all educated Hebrew readers. Here, for example, let me again mention the collection of proverbs, in the form of a *maqamah* (an Arabic prosimetric literary genre), titled *Fables from the Distant Past* by Isaac b. Solomon Ibn Sahula, written in 1281;[47] *Fox Fables* by R. Berechiah ha-Naqdan, in the thirteenth century;[48] and the much later anthology, titled Ḥidot de Izopeto ('*Las Fábulas de Ezopo*' or '*Aesop's Fables*') translated into Hebrew and Ladino by Avner Perez, with illustrations.[49]

Thus, *Tsemaḥ Tsaddik* joins two long and illustrious traditions. The dependence of *Tsemaḥ Tsaddik*, a Hebrew work, on the attributes of creatures that provide moral lessons, goes hand in hand with the tradition of the Hebrew folktale, and not only with the European folktale tradition, of which *Tsemaḥ Tsaddik* is also, naturally, a part.

38 | The Hebrew *Physiologus*

NOTES

1. Some of the English translations of biblical verses are taken from the Jewish Publication Society, *Tanakh: A New Translation of the Holy Scriptures According to the Traditional Hebrew Text* (Philadelphia PA: JPS, 1985); the rest are original translations from Hebrew by Ethelea Katzenell. Unless otherwise specified, all the Talmudic and Mishnaic quotations of the Jewish Sages are from the Babylonian Talmud. Most of the medieval rabbinic quotations in English translation are taken from 'Sefaria' online; the rest are original translations from Hebrew and Aramaic by Ethelea Katzenell. Any editorial comments embedded within biblical, talmudic, or other quotations, for the sake of clarification, appear within square brackets [...].

2. Vered Tohar, 'Reading L'*Ester* by Leon of Modena in the context of his other writings,' *Skené: Journal of Theatre and Drama Studies*, 9/1 (2023), 63–80. This article focuses on the interrelations between Modena's writings. Also see my book: Tohar, *The Hebrew Folktale in Pre-Modern Morality Literature* (Detroit MI: Wayne State University Press, 2023).

3. See Joseph Dan, *Hebrew Ethical and Homiletical Literature* (Jerusalem: Keter, 1974) [Hebrew]; Eli Yassif, 'The Hebrew story in the Middle Ages: An introduction', *Jewish Studies Quarterly*, 20/1 (2013), 3–8; also Isaiah Tishby and Joseph Dan (eds and anns) *Hebrew Ethical Literature: Selected Texts, with Introduction, Notes and Commentary: 10th–12th Centuries* (Jerusalem: M. Newman, 1970), pp. 11–24 [Hebrew].

4. See Zeev Gries, *The Book in the Jewish World, 1700–1900* (Portland OR: Littman Library of Jewish Civilization, 2010), pp. 46–56.

5. For more on Aristotelian ethics, see Timothy D. Roche, 'On the alleged metaphysical foundation of Aristotle's *Ethics*', *Ancient Philosophy*, 8/1 (Spring 1988), 49–62. More on Aristotelian poetics in George Whalley (trans. and ann.), *Aristotle's Poetics* (Montreal: McGill-Queen's University Press, 1997), pp. 72–92.

6. The text includes some revealing, personal confessions, such as his love of gambling and his bad economic decisions. For a scholarly edition of the text, see Mark R. Cohen (trans. and ed.), *The Autobiography of a Seventeenth-Century Venetian Rabbi* (Princeton NJ: Princeton University Press, 1988).

7. Michael Lambek, 'Toward an ethics of the act', in M. Lambek (ed.), *Ordinary Ethics: Anthropology, Language and Action* (New York: Fordham University Press, 2010), pp. 1–39.

Introduction | **39**

8. Veena Das, 'Ordinary ethics', in Didier Fassin (ed.), A *Companion to Moral Anthropology* (Chichester: Wiley-Blackwell, 2012), pp. 133–49.

9. For English see Aesop, *Aesop's Fables: English and Ancient Greek Edition*, selected and illustrated by Michael Hague (New York: Henry Holt & Co., 1985) [English/Greek].

10. Ron Baxter, *Bestiaries and Their Users in the Middle Ages* (London: Sutton, 1998), pp. 30–83.

11. On p. xvi of the Introduction, there is speculation regarding the identity of its author; for an English edition, see Michael J. Curley (trans.), *Physiologus (Naturalist): A Medieval Book of Nature Lore* (Austin TX: University of Texas Press, 1979); and 2nd edn (Chicago IL: Chicago University Press, 1979).

12. Originally written by Saint Isisdore in the early seventh century. Very few manuscript copies survived. First printed in 1472.

13. A manuscript written by Guillaume (William), Cleric of Normandy, *Le Bestiaire Divin (The Divine Bestiary)* (Normandy: c.1210); reprinted (Geneva: Slatkine Reprints, 1970) [French].

14. Recalling monastic *sensus spiritualis* ('spiritual sense') as discussed by Cardinal Henri de Lubac (1896–1991), in *Medieval Exegesis: The Four Senses of Scripture*, 3 vols, translated from French by Mark Sebanc and E. M. Macierowski (Grand Rapids MI: W. E. Eerdmans, 1998–2009); and Friedrich Ohly (1914–96), in *Sensus Spiritualis: Studies in Medieval Significs and the Philology of Culture*, translated from German by Kenneth J. Northcott (Chicago IL: University of Chicago Press, 2005).

15. The 1587 edition of the *Physiologus* was illustrated with accompanying wood-cut prints.

16. Moses (Moritz) Steinschneider, 'Jehuda (Leon) Modena und Fior di virtù', *Monatsschrift für Geschichte und Wissenschaft des Judentums*, 41(7) (1897), 324–6 [German]. For an English rendition of *Disciplina Clericalis*, see William Henry Hulme (trans.), *'Disciplina Clericalis (Training of the Clergy)*: English translation from the fifteenth century Worcester Cathedral Manuscript F–172', *Western Reserve Bulletin*, 22/3 (May 1919).

17. Emanuel Bin-Gorion, *In the Paths of the Talmudic Fables* (Jerusalem: Bialik Institute, 1970), p. 130 [Hebrew]. For an English version, see Christopher Stace (trans.), *Gesta Romanorum (Deeds of the Romans): A New Translation* (Manchester: Manchester University Press), 2016.

40 | The Hebrew *Physiologus*

18. Ann Jacobson Schutte, *Printed Italian Vernacular Religious Books, 1465–1550: A Finding List* (Geneva: Droz, 1983), p. 241. First printed in Venice or Milano 1471, and the first illustrated edition published in Venice 1487. Here, I used the 1856 Florentine edition, from the Harvard Library, based on an Italian manuscript from c. 1400; see Agenore Gelli, *Fiore di Virtù: Testo di Lingua Ridotto a Corretta Lezione* ('*Flower of Virtue: Text of Reduced Language and a Correct Lesson*') (Florence: F. Le Monnier, 1856) [Italian]. For the sake of comparison, I also used an English translation, based on a later Florentine edition, Nicholas Fersin (trans.), *The Florentine Fior di Virtù of 1491: An English Translation* (Washington, DC: Library of Congress, 1953).

19. See Dorit Raines, 'The Jews in the eyes of the Venetian patriarchy', in David Malkiel (ed.), *The Lion Shall Roar: R. Yehudah Modena and His World* (Jerusalem: Magnes Press, 2003), pp. xix–liv and 19–54 [Hebrew].

20. A comparison of the contents of an Italian edition of *Fiore di Virtù* (Florence, 1491) with the contents of first Hebrew edition of *Tsemaḥ Tsaddik* (Venice, 1600). Note that the chapter numbers and titles cited here come from the original Italian and do not always correspond to the chapter numbers and titles as they appear in the Hebrew version of *Tsemaḥ Tsaddi*.

21. Compare to Hebrew biblical verses (Genesis 4: 1–8).

22. Compare to Hebrew biblical verses (II Samuel 11: 1–17).

23. Compare to Hebrew biblical verses (Exodus 14: 5–30).

24. Compare to Hebrew biblical verses (Genesis 19: 1–38).

25. Compare to Hebrew biblical verses (Judges 16: 4–30).

26. Compare to Hebrew biblical verses (Genesis 6: 1–4).

27. Compare to Hebrew biblical verses (Genesis 3: 15–19).

28. Compare to Hebrew biblical verses (Genesis, Chapters 1–2), and note the biblical verse inserted into this tale, that comes from the story of 'Noah and the flood', found later in the Book of Genesis (9: 1–2).

29. The general name of this genre refers to all the anthologies of quotations, maxims, sayings and idioms on various topics, such as: *proverbial*, a popular sub-genre of collected medieval maxims, especially those in Latin; see also Barry Taylor, 'Medieval proverb collections: The west European tradition', *Journal of the Warburg and Courtauld Institute*, 55 (1992), 19–35.

Introduction | **41**

30. Maryanne C. Horwitz, *Seeds of Virtue and Knowledge* (Princeton NJ: Princeton University Press, 1998), pp. 103–5.

31. See Genesis 2: 16–17: 'And the Lord God commanded the man, saying: "Of every tree in the Garden you are free to eat; but as for the Tree of Knowledge of good and bad, you must not eat of it; for as soon as you eat of it, you shall die".' Also Genesis 3: 2–7: 'The woman replied to the serpent: "We may eat of the fruit of the other trees ... It is only about the fruit of the tree in the middle of the Garden that God said: 'You shall not eat of it or touch it, lest you die.'" And the serpent said to the woman: "You are not going to die, but God knows that as soon as you eat of it your eyes will be opened and you will be like divine beings who know good and bad." When the woman saw that the Tree was good for eating, and a delight to the eyes, and that the Tree was desirable as a source of wisdom, she took of its fruit and ate. She also gave some to her husband, and he ate. Then, the eyes of both of them were opened and they perceived that they were naked; and they sewed together fig leaves and made themselves loincloths.'

32. For more on this genre, see Curt Wachsmuth, *Studien zu des griechischen Florilegien* ('*Studies on the Greek "Flower Gathering"*') (Berlin: Weldmann, 1882) [German]; and Theodor Sherman, *Die Geschichte der dogmatischen Florilegien vom 5. bis 8 Jahrhundert* ('*The History of the Dogmatic "Flower Gathering" from the 5th–8th Century*') (Leipzig: J.C. Hinrichs, 1904) [German]; also Thomas Oestreich, *Florilegia* ('*Gathering Flowers*'): *The Catholic Encyclopedia*, vol. 6. (New York: Robert Appleton Co., 1909).

33. And has the connection between the act of learning and youth. According to Eliezer Ben-Yehudah's *Complete Dictionary of Ancient and Modern Hebrew*, vol. 10 (Jerusalem: Thomas Yosseloff, 1960), p. 5154 [Hebrew], the Hebrew noun *perah* (lit., 'flower') refers to any young human or animal (even another Hebrew term from the same root, *efro'ah* means 'chick' or 'hatchling'). Ben-Yehudah brings two phrases as examples: *pirhey kehunah* (young acolytes of the *Kohamin*, Jerusalem Temple priests, i.e., priests in training) (*cf.* tractate *Yoma* 1: 7) and *pirhey Livyah* (*Levi'im*, i.e., young Levite acolytes). See also the popular modern usage of the word *perah*, meaning a young trainee, a novice in an educational course; for example, *pirhey tayis* ('airforce cadets') and *perah hora'ah* ('student teacher'), etc.

34. Horwitz, *Seeds of Virtue and Knowledge*, pp. 103–5.

42 | The Hebrew *Physiologus*

35. The story titled 'The Barber who did not murder the Caesar thanks to a philosopher'.

36. The story titled 'The strange deeds of the angel'.

37. See, for example, the differences between Modena's version and that found in tractate *Sanhedrin* 107a: 2, found in Chapter 31 on 'fickleness' and 'King David's failure'.

38. See Rita Copeland, *Emotion and the History of Rhetoric in the Middle Ages* (Oxford: Oxford University Press, 2021).

39. To that end, Modena added a few wood-cut prints to replace the originals, see Shalom Sabar, 'A straight path before a painter: Leon Modena's attitude towards visual art', in David Malkiel (ed.), *The Lion Shall Roar: Leon Modena and His World* (Jerusalem: Magnes Press, 2003), pp. 163–92 [Hebrew].

40. *Vite dei santi Padri* was rendered into Italian vernacular in 1330 by a Dominican Friar named Domenico Cavalca at the Santa Caterina Monastery in the Sinai Desert. It was a translation of the original Latin, titled *Vitae Patrum* ('*Lives of the Fathers*') from the third and fourth centuries. See Domenico Cavalca (trans.) and Carlo Delcorno (ann.), *Vite dei santi Padri*, critical edn (Firenze: Sismel Edizioni del Galluzzo, 2009) [Italian].

41. The Hebrew version was printed, for example, in Nisim Shoshan, *Book of Tales, Sermons, and Legends* (Venice: Daniel Zaniti, 1600) [Hebrew], printed at the same time and place as *Tsemah Tsaddik*, making it highly likely that Modena knew the Jewish version.

42. For more on this, see Joanna Weinberg, 'Leon Modena and the *Fiore di Virtù*', in David Malkiel (ed.), *The Lion Shall Roar: Leon Modena and His World* (Jerusalem: Magnes Press, 2003), pp. 137–57, especially p. 140, fn. 15, where she claims that it is a fact that the researchers of the *Fiore di Virtù* are, usually, unaware that it has an adapted Hebrew translation.

43. Jacob Druckerman (ed.), 'Introduction', in *Tsemah Tsaddik: Melamed enosh binah ve-hokhmah, be-ma'alot ha-midot ve-hodam, me-Yehudah Aryeh Modena* ('*Righteous Growth: Teaches Human Wisdom, on the Degrees of the Virtues and Their Magnificence, by Judah Leon Modena*'), rev. edn (New York: A. H. Rozenberg, 1899), pp. xii–xiii [Hebrew].

44. As Raines showed in 'Judaism in the eyes of the Venetian patriarchy', pp. 19–54.

45. See also, Yair Zakovitch, 'Between *Aesop's Fables* and Hebrew biblical literature', *Yeda 'Am*, 20/47–8 (1981), 3–9 [Hebrew].

46. Haim Schwarzbaum, 'Rabbinic proverbs and *Aesop's Fables*', *Mahanayim*, 112 (1967), 12–17 [Hebrew].
47. See the scientific edition by Revital Refael-Vivante, *A Treasury of Fables: Isaac ibn Sahula's Meshal ha-Qadmoni (Fables from the Distant Past) (Castile, 1281): Text and Subtext* (Ramat-Gan: Bar-Ilan University Press, 2017) [Hebrew].
48. The illustrated edition, Haim Schwarzbaum, *Mishle Shu'alim (Fox Fables) of Rabbi Berechiah ha-Nakdan: A Study in Comparative Folklore and Fable Lore*, illustrated edn (Kiron: Institute for Jewish and Arab Folklore Research, 1979); Tamás Visi, 'Berechiah b. Natronai ha-Naqdan's *Dodi ve-Nekdi* (*My Uncle and My Grandson*) and the transfer of scientific knowledge from Latin to Hebrew in the twelfth century', *Historical Studies in Science and Judaism*, 14/2 (2014), 9–73; Tovi Bibring, 'In ictu oculi (In the blink of an eye): Reflections on wolf and beast by Berechiah ha-Naqdan in the context of its contemporary versions', *Comparative Literature Studies*, 56/2 (2019), 374–401; and Bibring, 'Would that my words were inscribed: Berechiah ha-Naqdan's *Mishlei Shu'alim (Fox Fables)* and European fable tradition', in Resianne Fontaine and Gad Freudenthal (eds), *Latin-into-Hebrew: Studies and Texts, volume 1: Studies* (Leiden: Brill Academic, 2013), pp. 309–29 [Latin/Hebrew]; as well as Revital Refael-Vivante, 'Charity as a value and norm in *Mishlei Shu'alim (Fox Fables)* by Rabbi Berechiah ha-Naqdan', in Tamás Visi, Tovi Bibring and Daniel Soukup (eds), *Berechiah ben Natronai ha-Naqdan's Works and Their Reception* (Turnhout: Brepols, 2019), pp. 53–74 [English/Hebrew].
49. See Avner Perez (trans.), *Hidot de Izopeto* ('Las Fábulas de Ezopo'; '*Aesop's Fables*') (Ma'aleh Adumim: Ma'aleh Adumim Institute for the Documentation of the Ladino Language and its Culture, 2007) [Hebrew/Ladino]; also see David Rotman, 'Author and fiction, lamb and wolf: Hebrew adaptations of *Aesop's Fables* from the Middle Ages through the early modern era', *Te'udah*, 28 (2017), 495–537 [Hebrew].

44 | The Hebrew *Physiologus*

WORKS CITED

Aesop, *Aesop's Fables: English and Ancient Greek Edition*, selected and illustrated by Michael Hague (New York: Henry Holt & Co., 1985) [English/Greek].

Baxter, Ron, *Bestiaries and Their Users in the Middle Ages* (London: Sutton, 1998).

Ben-Yehudah, Eliezer, *Complete Dictionary of Ancient and Modern Hebrew*, vol. 10 (Jerusalem: Thomas Yosseloff, 1960) [Hebrew].

Bibring, Tovi, 'In ictu oculi (In the blink of an eye): Reflections on wolf and beast by Berechiah ha-Naqdan in the context of its contemporary versions', *Comparative Literature Studies*, 56/2 (2019), 374–401.

Bibring, Tovi, 'Would that my words were inscribed: Berechiah ha-Naqdan's *Mišhlei Šhu'alim* (*Fox Fables*) and European fable tradition', in Resianne Fontaine and Gad Freudenthal (eds), *Latin-into-Hebrew: Studies and Texts, Volume 1: Studies* (Leiden: Brill Academic, 2013) [Latin/Hebrew].

Bin-Gorion, Emanuel, *In the Paths of the Talmudic Fables* (Jerusalem: Bialik Institute, 1970) [Hebrew].

Cavalca, Domenico (trans.) and Carlo Delcorno (ann.), *Vite dei santi Padri* (*'Lives of the Sainted Fathers'*), critical edn (Firenze: Sismel Edizioni del Galluzzo, 2009) [Italian].

Cohen, Mark R. (trans. and ed.), *The Autobiography of a Seventeenth-Century Venetian Rabbi: Leon Modena's Life of Judah* (Princeton NJ: Princeton University Press, 1988).

Copeland, Rita, *Emotion and the History of Rhetoric in the Middle Ages* (Oxford: Oxford University Press, 2021).

Curley, Michael J. (trans.), *Physiologus: A Medieval Book of Nature Lore* (Austin TX: University of Texas Press, 1979); 2nd edn (Chicago IL: Chicago University Press, 1979).

Dan, Joseph, *Hebrew Ethical and Homiletical Literature* (Jerusalem: Keter, 1974) [Hebrew].

Dan, Joseph, *The Hebrew Story in the Middle Ages: Studies of its History* (Jerusalem: Keter, 1974) [Hebrew].

Das, Veena, 'Ordinary ethics', in Didier Fassin (ed.), *A Companion to Moral Anthropology* (Chichester: Wiley-Blackwell, 2012), pp. 133–49.

De Lubac, Henri, *Medieval Exegesis: The Four Senses of Scripture*, 3 vols, trans. by Mark Sebanc and Edward M. Macierowski (Grand Rapids MI: W. E. Eerdmans, 1998–2009).

Druckerman, Jacob (ed.), 'Introduction', Tsemaḥ Tsaddik: Melamed enosh binah ve-ḥokhmah, be-ma'alot ha-midot ve-hodam, me-Yehudah Aryeh Modena ('Righteous Growth: Teaches Human Wisdom, on the Degrees of the Virtues and Their Magnificence, by Judah Leon Modena'), revised edn (New York: A. H. Rozenberg, 1899), pp. xii–xiii [Hebrew].

Evans, Stephen, A History of Western Philosophy from the Pre-Socratics to Postmodernism (Westmont IL: IVP Academic, 2018).

Fersin, Nicholas (trans.), The Florentine Fior di Virtù of 1491: An English Translation (Washington, DC: Library of Congress, 1953).

Gelli, Agenore, Fiore di Virtù: Testo di Lingua Ridotto a Corretta Lezione ('Flower of Virtue: Text of Reduced Language and a Correct Lesson') (Florence: F. Le Monnier, 1856) [Italian].

Gries, Zeev, The Book in the Jewish World, 1700–1900 (Portland OR: Littman Library of Jewish Civilization, 2010).

Guillaume (William), Cleric of Normandy, Le Bestiaire Divin ('The Divine Bestiary') (Normandy: 1210 or 1211); reprinted (Geneva: Slatkine Reprints, 1970) [French].

Horwitz, Maryanne C., Seeds of Virtue and Knowledge (Princeton NJ: Princeton University Press, 1998).

Hulme, William Henry (trans.), 'Disciplina Clericalis (Training of the Clergy): English translation from the fifteenth century Worcester Cathedral Manuscript F–172', Western Reserve Bulletin, 22/3 (May 1919).

Ibn Gabirol, Solomon, The Improvement of the Moral Qualities, trans. by Stephen S. Wise (New York: AMS Press, 1966) [Arabic/English].

Jewish Publication Society, Tanakh: A New Translation of the Holy Scriptures According to the Traditional Hebrew Text (Philadelphia: JPS, 1985).

Lambek, Michael, 'Toward an Ethics of the Act', in Ordinary Ethics: Anthropology, Language and Action (New York: Fordham University Press, 2010), pp. 1–39.

Malkiel, David (ed.), The Lion Shall Roar: Leon Modena and His World (Jerusalem: Magnes Press, 2003), pp. xii–xiii [Hebrew/English].

Modena, Yehudah Aryeh, Tsemaḥ Tsaddik ('Righteous Growth') (Venice: Daniel Zaniti, 1600) [Hebrew].

Oestreich, Thomas, Florilegia ('Gathering Flowers'): The Catholic Encyclopedia, vol. 6 (New York: Robert Appleton Co., 1909).

46 | The Hebrew *Physiologus*

Ohly, Friedrich, *Sensus Spiritualis: Studies in Medieval Significs and the Philology of Culture*, trans. from German by Kenneth J. Northcott (Chicago IL: University of Chicago Press, 2005).

Perez, Avner (trans.), *Ḥidot de Izopeto* ('*Las Fábulas de Ezopo*'; '*Aesop's Fables*') (Ma'aleh Adumim: Ma'aleh Adumim Institute for the Documentation of the Ladino Language and Its Culture, 2007) [Hebrew/Ladino].

Raines, Dorit, 'The Jews in the eyes of the Venetian patriarchy in the time of R. Yehudah Aryeh of Modena', in David Malkiel (ed.), *The Lion Shall Roar: R. Yehudah Modena and His World* (Jerusalem: Magnes Press, 2003), pp. xix–liv and 19–54 [Hebrew].

Refael-Vivante, Revital, *A Treasury of Fables: Isaac ibn Sahula's Meshal ha-Qadmoni (Fables from the Distant Past) (Castile, 1281): Text and Subtext* (Ramat-Gan: Bar-Ilan University Press, 2017) [Hebrew].

Refael-Vivante, Revital, 'Charity as a value and norm in *Mishlei Shu'alim (Fox Fables)* by Rabbi Berechiah ha-Naqdan', in Tamás Visi, Tovi Bibring and Daniel Soukup (eds), *Berechiah ben Natronai ha-Naqdan's Works and Their Reception* (Turnhout: Brepols, 2019), pp. 53–74 [English/Hebrew].

Roche, Timothy D., 'On the alleged metaphysical foundation of Aristotle's Ethics', *Ancient Philosophy*, 8/1 (Spring 1988), 49–62.

Rotman, David, 'Author and fiction, lamb and wolf: Hebrew adaptations of *Aesop's Fables* from the Middle Ages through the early modern era', *Te'udah*, 28 (2017), 495–537 [Hebrew].

Sabar, Shalom, '"A straight path before a painter": Leon Modena's attitude towards visual art', in David Malkiel (ed.), *The Lion Shall Roar: Leon Modena and His World* (Jerusalem: Magnes Press, 2003), pp.163–92 [Hebrew].

Schutte, Ann Jacobson, *Printed Italian Vernacular Religious Books, 1465–1550: A Finding List* (Geneva: Droz, 1983).

Schwarzbaum, Ḥaim, *Mishle Shu'alim (Fox Fables) of Rabbi Berechiah ha-Nakdan: A Study in Comparative Folklore and Fable Lore* (Kiron: Institute for Jewish and Arab Folklore Research, 1979).

Schwarzbaum, Ḥaim, 'Rabbinic proverbs and *Aesop's Fables*', *Maḥanayim*, 112 (1967), 12–17 [Hebrew].

Sherman, Theodor, *Die Geschichte der dogmatischen Florilegien vom 5. bis 8 Jahrhundert* (*'The History of the Dogmatic "Flower Gathering" from the 5th–8th Century'*) (Leipzig: J.C. Hinrichs, 1904) [German].

Shoshan, Nisim, *Book of Tales, Sermons, and Legends* (Venice: Daniel Zaniti, 1600) [Hebrew].

Stace, Christopher (trans.), *Gesta Romanorum* (*Deeds of the Romans*): A New *Translation* (Manchester: Manchester University Press), 2016.

Steinschneider, Moses (Moritz), 'Jehuda (Leon) Modena und Fior di virtù', *Monatsschrift für Geschichte und Wissenschaft des Judentums*, 41/7 (1897), 324–6 [German].

Taylor, Barry, 'Medieval proverb collections: The west European tradition', *Journal of the Warburg and Courtauld Institute*, 55 (1992), 19–35.

Tishby, Isaiah, and Joseph Dan (eds and anns), *Hebrew Ethical Literature: Selected Texts, with Introduction, Notes and Commentary: 10th–12th Centuries* (Jerusalem: M. Newman, 1970) [Hebrew], pp. 11–24.

Tohar, Vered, 'Reading L'*Ester* by Leon of Modena in the context of his other writings', *Skené: Journal of Theatre and Drama Studies*, 9/1 (2023), 63–80.

Tohar, Vered, *The Hebrew Folktale in Pre-Modern Morality Literature* (Detroit MI: Wayne State University Press, 2023).

Visi, Tamás, 'Berechiah ben Naṭronai ha-Naqdan's *Dodi ve-Neḵdi* (*My Uncle and My Grandson*) and the transfer of scientific knowledge from Latin to Hebrew in the twelfth century', *Historical Studies in Science and Judaism*, 14/2 (2014), 9–73.

Wachsmuth, Curt, *Studien zu des griechischen Florilegien* (*'Studies on the Greek "Flower Gathering"'*) (Berlin: Weldmann, 1882) [German].

Whalley, George (trans. and ann.), *Aristotle's Poetics* (Montreal: McGill-Queen's University Press, 1997).

Weinberg, Joanna, 'Leon Modena and the *Fiore di Virtù*', in David Malkiel (ed.), *The Lion Shall Roar: Leon Modena and His World* (Jerusalem: Magnes Press, 2003), pp. 137–57.

Yassif, Eli, 'The Hebrew story in the Middle Ages: An introduction', *Jewish Studies Quarterly*, 20/1 (2013), 3–8.

Zakovitch, Yair, 'Between *Aesop's Fables* and Hebrew biblical literature,' *Yeda 'Am*, 20/47–8 (1981), 3–9 [Hebrew].

THE TEXT[50]

CHAPTER I
ON THE VIRTUE OF LOVE, IN GENERAL

OUR SAGES recognised the integrity of love and affection, and knew about love's magnificence from many books that rightly guide and teach its ways. They said that it starts by knowing the beloved object, since no one can love something unknown. Such knowledge may arrive by means of one of the five primary senses in the body: seeing through the eyes; hearing with the ears; smelling through the nose; tasting in the mouth; and touching with the hands. However, this knowledge may also be received via a more respectable means than the physical body – coming from the mind, created by the intellect. Such knowledge is the primary cause and marks the beginning of love. Usually, humans become aware of love through their eyes, as the researcher (Aristotle) wrote in his book *On Sense and the Sensible* (350 BCE), because people's desire is stirred by such awareness. Then, memory will awaken and recall that pleasure. Later, imagining that pleasurable object that had been brought to

---

50. See *www.anzarouth.com/2009/08/tzemach-1-love-general.html* (last accessed 10 June 2024).

50 | The Hebrew *Physiologus*

mind would arouse lust in the heart, causing people to covet that which they had desired for themselves. As a result, the excellent and important virtue of 'love' would be born, becoming the root, the basis and the key – as the philosopher said – to all the other virtues, all of which originated from love. King Solomon told us to love morality and love knowledge, as if saying that morality and knowledge will emanate from those who love. Likewise, the speech of the pure-hearted lover is graceful and dignified, and the objects of that love will attest that the speaker is indeed pure-hearted, clean-spoken and pure in both deed and society. In the Song of Songs, love is redoubled and multiplied; there it is written that the beloved is decked with love. Talmudic tractate *Sanhedrin* (105b: 11), records a statement by R. Shim'on b. El'azar, that love nullifies Abraham, the Patriarch's greatness, as described (Genesis 19: 27), since Abraham arose early in the morning and rushed to saddle his ass, meaning that love is the highest virtue, because it removes pride, standing above all that is more trivial, purifying the heart, preparing the devoted lover with agility and cleanliness. For God called our forefather Abraham: 'Abraham, my love' for his unwavering love; Abraham had set aside his own dignity, making haste to do God's bidding by himself. As such, they who wish to know how this virtue differs from the lacking and the indecent should first contemplate why they want to be swayed by the virtue of love – laying bare the plain facts of each act, whether it is good or bad.

And we can continue to describe the virtue of love as being like a bird flying over the Land of Israel, the one that the foreigners call *Caladrius*, that when brought to the bedside of the severely ill, turns its head away from the terminally ill, not wanting to see them, but gazes steadily at those who will survive. Similarly, pure-hearted lovers cannot bear to do or see anything vile, and will cease and always dwell in ways of goodness and morality, in the company of the generous of heart, those like the cedars of Lebanon, where birds nest, where they will display the most perfect energy in times of sorrow and grief, more so than

Caladrius.
From chapter 1, 'On the virtue of love, in general'.

in times of joy and rejoicing – like a burning candle that lights the darkness and the gloom, more than it does in the light and sunlight – because when it has reason to change its course, it proves the purity of its love.

Nonetheless, we must know the order and degrees of love because Humanity must first love its Creator above all else, as written (Deuteronomy 6: 5): 'Love God with all your heart and soul!' even if it costs you your life. Then, your father and mother, for whom God also commanded (Leviticus 19: 3): 'Revere your mother and father!' and especially love those mandated by nature. Then, for fellow humans, as written (Leviticus 19: 18): 'Love all others as yourself', and those in your country – all individuals according to their level – since the righteous are worthy of more love than the wicked, although even the wicked are entitled to love, to reform them, as stated: 'May sins cease to exist in the [Holy] Land, the sins, not the sinners, whose deeds must be amended'. Thus, following the aforementioned order for loving, the last discussed is the love for women.

CHAPTER 2
ON THE LOVE OF GOD

THE 'LOVE OF GOD' arises in humans after the promotion of two qualities – faith and hope. In other words, a person cannot love God if he or she does not believe in the existence of an eternal, living God, the one and only, the first and last. Therefore, it begins with acceptance of the yoke ('authority') of the divine kingdom (Deuteronomy 6: 4): 'Hear, O Israel, the Lord is our God, the Lord is one!' And, after we admit that God is real and singular, we say: 'Love God!' And, indeed, we must also have hope and a sense of purpose for joining God and enjoying the glorious Divine Presence, since these two qualities breed an intensely strong love of God in people, until the mundane delights of the world do not compare with the desire to do God's bidding, as is written in Ecclesiastes (1: 13): 'I set my heart to study and explore with wisdom'; (Ecclesiastes 2: 4–5): 'I built myself houses and I planted vineyards. I made myself gardens and groves'. Yet, Ecclesiastes

Bat.
From chapter 39, 'On adultery'.

also recognised (2: 11) that 'It was all futile'. As in the words of the Song of Songs (8: 7): 'Vast floods cannot quench the love, nor can rivers wash it away. Even if a man offered all his household's wealth for love, he would be laughed at and scorned.' In his love of God, Abraham, the Patriarch, was willing to sacrifice his only son, and tied him to the sacrificial alter. Many of the original pious ('Hassidim') gave their lives (were martyred) out of love for the sanctity of God, the most prominent being Rabbi 'Akiva, discussed at length. After a royal edict had been issued banning the study of *Torah*, R. 'Akiva continued to gather Jews in public, was caught and flayed by iron combs. All the while, he was happy and recited the 'Hear, O Israel' prayer until, with his last breath, he spoke the final word 'one!' He, like others, studied and knew the world's vanities, the lack of respect for others, how people belittled others to make themselves feel bigger, those who could not feel rich unless others were poor. What does this resemble? A large table with a small, short tablecloth on it, that all those seated around the table are trying to pull to their place, thus uncovering that of another – until putting God's love into this world, one will eat and cry throughout life, but those who love God reveal it and are ever joyful. In tractate *Sotah* (31a: 8), R. Shim'on b. El'azar stated: 'Greater is the one who performs *mitsvot* [God's commandments] out of love than the one who performs them out of fear.' It is written (Exodus 20: 6) that God was benevolent to the loving generations and to those who kept the divine commandments. There, it also said that two students were sitting with Rava, and one student said that he dreamt that they had read to him (Psalms 31: 20): 'How abundant is the good that You have in store for those who fear You.' And the other said that he dreamt (Psalms 5: 12): 'Let all those who take refuge in You rejoice forever.' Rava told them they were both completely righteous, 'between love and reverence', and that, 'rejoice forever' refers to the lovers of God, since the end of that verse says: 'let those who love Your name exult in You'; their sufferings in this world are transient and mild, while their eternal rewards await in the everlasting world ('afterlife') – blessed are they who wait and get their due.

54 | The Hebrew *Physiologus*

CHAPTER 3
ON THE LOVE OF FATHER, MOTHER AND RELATIVES

THE SECOND VIRTUE is ('familial love') people's love of their fathers, mothers and all their relatives – their own flesh and blood. Nature bends the will to prioritise love of family before that of others. And we know the magnitude of the obligation to love and respect our parents, as Solomon said (Proverbs 15: 20): 'A wise son makes his father happy, a fool of a man humiliates his mother.' As said, that it was very beneficial for Esau that he respected Isaac and Rebecca above other people. In tractate *Kiddushin* it reads: 'Go and see what one gentile did in Ashkelon, named Dama b. Netina.' The sages once asked him to get gemstones for a breastplate in return for a fee of sixty *ribo*, but the (access) key was under the head of his sleeping father, whom he refused to trouble. The following year, God granted him a reward – the birth of a rare red heifer in his herd. When the sages met with Dama, he told them: 'I know that any sum I'd ask for, you'd give me. However, I ask only that you pay me the same sum that I forfeited out of respect for my father.' When the sages heard this, they responded: 'What is he who does not demand this – how much more so is he who makes such a demand as this!' Afterwards, they were able to love his brother and relatives, because the sages had already said that none are poorer than those lacking blood-relatives because, in the end, blood never turns to water, and people should always help and save one another in times of need. Our Rabbis also stated in tractate *Yevamot* (62b: 19): 'One who loves his neighbours, and who draws his relatives close.' And those who loan a *sela* coin ('ancient silver tetradrachm'), to someone poor in a time of need, it is said of them (Isaiah 58: 9): 'Then, when you call, the Lord will answer when you cry. He will say: "Here I am!"' And your poor and the poor in your city – yours come first since the soul is in the blood.

CHAPTER 4
ON FRIENDSHIP

THE THIRD VIRTUE is also a type of love – 'friendship', peace and brotherhood. It is to placate each other by words of truth and justice. And this love provides the basis for amiable and polite social interaction that people value. However, the reason for this is one of three. First, for the (personal) goodness and benefits people may hope to gain one from another, that in all love that is dependent on something, when that 'something' is voided, love dies, having become diminished, gone bad. Second, for the (mutual) benefits that they would provide each other, like two hands washing each other, this type of love is deemed 'good'. And third, when the lover seeks to benefit the beloved, no matter what, even if this causes personal damage and loss, this type of love is 'total love' and there is none higher. The experience of such total

Beaver.
From chapter 10, *'On peace'.*

56 | The Hebrew *Physiologus*

love is only when the lover is wholehearted and will try to do anything and everything to please and protect the beloved from all things bad or harmful. The lover's relationship and standing are acquired and maintained by three things: the respect given to the beloved, both in his or her presence and in his or her absence and by the assistance proffered to the beloved in times of need – not only during successful times, after which the (fickle) lover flees or distances himself or herself in troubled times. For it is known that (in tractate *Shabbat*, R. Papa said): 'At the entrance of a store, many brethren and lovers stand, but at a shameful place, there are no brethren or lovers.' And it is also known that the crown of loyal, loving couples were David and Jonathan, whose marvellous love is written in the Hebrew Scriptures (I Samuel 18: 1 and 3), about their lives and deaths. A sage said, 'Four things are better when they are older than when they are new: wine, fish, oil, and love most of all'. Aristotle stated that the bigger the tree, the more sustenance it requires, just as great personages need many lovers, since no one in this world is happy alone, only in the company of friends; as (Rava said in tractate *Ta'anit*, 23a: 18), 'Either friendship or death'. Thus, the philosopher Arachytas said that, if a man were to go up into the sky and see the Sun, its origin and the entire span of its lifetime, and the beauty of the Moon and the stars in their celestial paths, and would then come back down and see the glory of the Earth and all it has – that man would not experience joy, but rather great sorrow, if he were alone and could not tell his close, personal friends. As written (in tractate *Berakhot* 17a): 'It is commonly said that a man is always naked in the fear [of God], answering softly, responding warmly, spending time with siblings, and relatives, and even foreigners in the marketplace, to incur God's favour, by being nice below and amenable to all God's creations.' They adjured – Always remember that people tend to conform with beloved companions. Therefore (in tractate *Avot* 1: 6) R. Joshua b. Praḥyah commands: 'Acquire a [good] friend!' Seneca used to say that before choosing people to love, study them, test them, and after that experience – love them with all your heart!

In ancient Roman texts, we read that the King of Sicily had sentenced a man named Pythias to death by beheading. Pythias petitioned the king to grant him eight days so that he might go home, make a last will and put his affairs in order. The king taunted Pythias, saying he would grant the stay of execution only if Pythias found someone who would agree to sit in jail and forfeit his head in Pythias' stead, lest he not return before the agreed on eight days came to an end. So, Pythias sent for his beloved friend, named Damon, a soulmate, who also loved him very much, and Pythias told Damon about the help he needed. Damon went immediately to the king and agreed to be beheaded if Pythias did not return within the allotted eight days; so, Damon was imprisoned until Pythias would return. The designated time was approaching, but Pythias had not yet returned, and the public was insulting Damon for making that commitment; but Damon was not afraid at all, because he believed, with all his heart, in his trustworthy, beloved friend. And, indeed, at the end of the allotted time, Pythias returned, honouring his oath. When the king saw Damon's enormous love and loyalty to Pythias, he no longer wanted to put him to death, so as not to part two such perfect lovers.

CHAPTER 5
ON NATURAL LOVE

THE FOURTH VIRTUE is 'natural love', that cannot be controlled by human will, because nature forces and steers us to love what is like us: in substance, in form and in deed, seen through the eyes and found to have appealing actions, whether good or bad; a love at first sight, without receiving any pleasure or benefit.

This is exemplified by observing mindless animals that love animals like themselves, as explained (in tractate Bava Kama 93: 2): 'Each raven dwells with its own species', even if it gets nothing from them. Similarly, all those who share a certain artistry will naturally love one another, although an artist that is jealous of a fellow artist will hate someone who shares the same talent. Such love results from fear that others might do harm or become envious. Plato said that if you seek that which is like yourself, look to those who love you without cause. Our sages have already hinted: 'Why did the starling follow the crow? Because it was of the same kind' (as in the famous English proverb, 'Birds of a feather flock together').

Starling and crow.
From chapter 5, 'On natural love'.

CHAPTER 6
ON THE LOVE OF WOMEN

THE FIFTH VIRTUE is the most exciting, and is entirely physical, most of which is primarily the 'love of women', also connoted as 'bad' and 'good', depending on the intended purpose. This has drawn many people to speak at length, some in reproach of women, others in their praise. And this may be interpreted to mean that some love women only for the pleasure they take with them, which is animalistic lust, dependent on the physical senses, especially the sense of touch; this we consider disgraceful, because it neither notices nor thinks about harm (to the women), nor about the advantages of respect or shame, and the disadvantage or completion of what is done. In this regard, King Solomon said (Ecclesiastes 7: 26): 'Now, I find the woman more bitter than death, who is all traps, snares.' And the sages said (in tractate *Shabbat*): 'A woman is a skin-bottle full of faeces and her mouth is full of blood, yet everyone runs after her.' They want to remind us that the first woman (Eve) caused death in the world, though the sages verbally abused only the bad women. One philosopher said that three things chase a man out of his home: smoke, emptiness and a bad wife. Hippocrates said to a woman carrying fire in her hands: 'Here's fire carrying fire, but the fire of the porter burns more than the fire being carried.' Avicenna said to a woman who was learning how to write: 'Why add bad to bad?' However, of a man who loves a decent woman for the purpose of sacred procreation, we would say, as it is written (Genesis 29: 18): 'Jacob loved Rachel.' And the essence of such love is in the mind and thoughts. Indeed, as we know, Solomon provided an example in his Song of Songs. By means of God's love, a pious man will learn about her from her physical attributes. Since, a righteous man truly loves God, as he loves a woman, he is unable to sleep, to eat, to drink, and is steadfast through scorching heat by

60 | The Hebrew *Physiologus*

Cranes.
From chapter 2, 'On loyalty'.

day and frost by night in her love. As written in *Bereshit Rabbah*, R. Shim'on said: 'God expressed affection for [the People of] Israel in three ways: attraction, desire and aspiration.' And we learn about 'attraction' from the affair of that wicked man Shekhem b. Ḥamor in Genesis (34: 2, 8 and 19): '[Shekhem] ... was strongly drawn to Dinah, daughter of Jacob.' 'Desire' – 'My son longs for your daughter.' 'Aspiration' – 'for he wanted Jacob's daughter.' R. Abba b. Elisha' added another pair: 'by means of love and conversation.' In regard to suitable love, Solomon said (Proverbs 18: 22): 'He who finds a wife has found happiness.' And (Proverbs 5: 18): 'Find joy in the wife of your youth.' It is also written in the *Book of Ben Sira*: 'A good woman is a good gift.' As written (Psalms 128: 3): 'Your wife shall be like a fruitful vine within your house.' Happy are those who love intellectual, not emotional love, since that is what sets humans apart from the beasts. On this, it was written (Song of Songs 8: 6): 'Its sparks are sparks of fire, a divine flame.'

CHAPTER 7
ON ENVY

'ENVY', 'JEALOUSY' and 'covetousness' represent a vice contrary to love and peace, having two aspects – the first is regret when others benefit, that is, considering the success of others to be a bad thing; the second is enjoying the adversity that befalls others. Both are very bad, unless, like our prophets, they follow the path of regret, questioning why the wicked prosper or appreciating God's vengeance against our enemies. However, when the heart is full of such passion, from a bad heart, with only wickedness and malice, there is no worse vice than this.

The *Rishonim* [rabbis and scholars from the eleventh to fifteenth centuries] already stated that an envious person is worse than a covetous one, describing a king who approached the two and told them to each make any request they wish, and he would grant it. The covetous one asked that they give him double whatever the

Falcons.
From chapter 28, 'On largesse'.

other requested. The envious one asked that they pluck out one of his own eyes, just so they would pluck out both of his friend's eyes.

Let us compare the vice of envy to a certain bird called the Magpie said to be so envious that, if it saw that its chicks in the nest were fat, it would peck them in the ribs several times with its beak until they shed the fat and became thinner.

And Solomon, in his wisdom said (Proverbs 14: 30) that matrimony heals the heart, and envy rots the bones. In tractate *Shabbat* (152: 9), a tale is told about gravediggers in reference to two verses, one in Ecclesiastes (12: 7) and the other in Proverbs (14: 30) – 'Passion is rot to the bones'. The bones of anyone filled with jealousy will rot. It is said (Job 5: 2) that 'Vexation kills the fool and envy murders the simpleton'. A sage said, 'Where there is jealousy, there cannot be love'; so even if you want to take revenge on the one envious of you, avoid evil (do not do evil deeds) and do good. Envy makes your neighbours' wheat crops appear more plentiful than yours. How can someone successful be safe from envy? It has been said that people should be more wary of the jealousy of relatives and loved ones than of enemies. This caused the breaking of the pact of the first brothers in the world, Cain and Abel, because, from Cain's perspective (Genesis 4: 4–5), 'The Lord paid heed to Abel and his offering, but to Cain and his offering He paid no heed'. The fire of envy burnt in Cain, who rose up against his brother and killed him, thus becoming the first murderer. The first blood spilled on the land was pure and righteous blood.

CHAPTER 8
ON HAPPINESS

IN SHORT, 'happiness' is an outcome of love. It expresses composure and generosity, and the ability to experience healthy human pleasure. Solomon said (Proverbs 17: 22): 'A joyful heart makes for good health; despondency dries up the bones.' And one is, indeed, meant to take pleasure in love, with morality and goodness, and not enjoy the misfortune of others. As it is written (Proverbs 24: 17–18): 'If your enemy falls, do not exult; if he trips, let your heart not rejoice.' And it is not to be treated lightly, as R. 'Akiva would say (in tractate Avot 3: 13): 'Jesting and frivolity accustom a person to promiscuity.' One need only be satisfied with one's lot in life to feel wealthy; as stated in Avot (4: 1): 'Who is the rich one? He who is happy with his lot.' And one must rejoice in God, as written (Psalms 32: 11): 'Rejoice in the Lord and exult, O you righteous; shout for joy,

Wolf.
From chapter 16, 'On admonition'.

all upright men!' And as written (Psalms 105: 3): 'Let all who seek the Lord rejoice.' This is all in preparation for the Divine Spirit; the sages have said that prophecy can occur only in an atmosphere of joy. In tractate *Shabbat* it says (Ecclesiastes 8: 15): 'I, therefore, praise enjoyment.' This is the joy of fulfilling a commandment and, in all that is sacred (Psalms 14: 7): 'Jacob will exult, Israel will rejoice.'

In regard to this commandment (to be happy), our sages have told many tales, especially about the water libation celebration held in the Jerusalem Temple during the Tabernacles holiday, that anyone who had not seen that celebration, had never seen real joy. In tractate *Sukkah* (53a: 7), they spoke about R. Shim'on b. Gamliel, when he was happy at the water libation celebration; he would take eight flaming torches and throw them upwards, one by one, catching each one in turn. Then he would bow down, digging both his thumbs into the earth, kiss the ground and straighten up like no other living creature could. Similarly, King David also used to skip and dance about before the Holy Ark, saying (II Samuel 6: 22): 'I dishonour myself even more.' Our sages also commanded us to make brides and grooms happy. 'This is our God ... in whom we trust; let us rejoice and exult in His deliverance' (Isaiah 25: 9).

CHAPTER 9
ON WORRY

THE VICES of 'sadness' and 'worry' are contrary to (the virtue) of happiness; they are excessive sorrow, regarding something from the past, or anxiously awaiting something in the future. Sorrow about the past is called 'sadness', while concern regarding the future is 'worry' – and the two are inseparable – only when a person is sad about sins committed in the past, as David was (Psalms 6: 4): 'My whole being is stricken with terror' out of fear of sinning. Yet (Psalms 16: 8) says, 'I am ever mindful of the Lord's presence'; but since what was done cannot be undone, one should not have regrets and dwell on it. Our Rabbis said (*Mishnah Berakhot* 9: 3): 'A man, whose wife was pregnant, said: "May my wife deliver a baby boy!" This was a prayer made in vain [a sin in Judaism, since God had already determined the sex of the foetus]'; similar to the statement in tractate *Mo'ed Katan* (27b): 'Do not weep for the dead too much, nor lament more than a measured amount. Why? Three [days] for crying, seven for eulogising ... Anyone who grieves inconsolably over his dead will, in the end, weep for another person.' And regarding the future, the poet (Solomon) wrote about calm and confidence, because the terror will not be postponed, once it has been decreed. Solomon said (Proverbs 12: 25): 'If there is anxiety in a man's mind, let him quash it.' R. Solomon Ibn Gabirol, in his (Arabic) manuscript, *The Improvement of the Moral Qualities* (Saragossa, 1045), devoted his longest chapter to this vice, because it was the most likely to bring a person to Death's doorway.

And when Alexander the Great, King of Macedon heard from Aristotle that worry can smelt the human heart, destroying it, and Alexander wished to test the truth of it, he took some species of animals resembling humans by nature and locked them up for many days in the darkness, commanding that they be fed, so they

66 | The Hebrew *Physiologus*

would live. Afterwards, he took them out and slaughtered them and saw their hearts were entirely melted, thus confirming the truth of his mentor's claim.

Furthermore, it is written that worry comes and grows stronger in a person who is drunk on earthly possessions and delights, who counts them and what he lacks, or spends all his life in pain for fear of losing them. They asked Socrates: 'How is it that you never show any signs of worry?' He replied that he never acquired anything that would worry him if it disappeared. As such, it is fitting that everyone heeds Ptolemy's suggestion, that all who hope for longevity become bravehearted before such incidents occur.

One can take an example from the raven, which, after the birth of its hatchlings, which were white, became so very sad that it left them, thinking that they did not belong to it because they were not similar, not black, so it did not bring them food until their black feathers grew in. In any case, they survived on the dew, the air and, according to our sages, on the little mosquitoes that God sent them flying directly into their mouths, as written (Psalms 147: 9): '[The Lord ...] who gives ... the raven's brood what they cry for.' All this the raven does out of the sadness that controls him; thus, he grows sadder than all other living creatures, having lost his offspring.

In the *Book of Ben Sira* it says: 'Do not worry, because worry has killed many.' And Plato said that worry is unbecoming of a wise man. And Seneca stated that worry buries men, so do not take it to heart, for if you do fall into a worrisome state, do not let everyone see, because someone intelligent does not reveal all that is in his heart. Know that sadness is born of idleness; it is said that idleness breeds boredom and boredom is a cause for worry. One sage said that just as it is human nature to learn from much work, so much idleness yields foolishness; further-more, Ecclesiastes (2: 24) said: 'There is nothing worthwhile for a man but to eat and drink and afford himself enjoyment with his means [the fruit of his labours]', for his work is *Torah* ('study') and his job (Proverbs 31: 7): 'and forget their poverty and put troubles out of mind.' 'Cast your burden on the Lord and He will sustain you' (Psalms 55: 23); God will protect you from all evil and guard your soul.

Among the consolers on the labour of worry, it is written that when Alexander of Macedon died, he was carried in a gold casket on the shoulders of generous governors, military officers and philosophers, who walked and eulogised him. One said, 'The bravery of this ruler was worldwide, so he will be buried now in all the land, from East to West, on four square cubits'. Another said, 'Throughout Alexander's life, everyone was silent, but now everyone speaks, since he cannot speak'. Another spoke, 'Those who were covetous of you yesterday, comfort you today'. Many eulogised him. However, before his own death, Alexander wrote a letter of condolences to his mother that read:

Mother, when you hear of Alexander's death, command the restoration of a large and beautiful city and, there, prepare all the foods and drinks he would have. And gather around you all the people of the kingdom for a day of feasting. But make it known, lest someone attends the Queen's banquet who had suffered tribulations, that he should mourn Alexander differently than the grieving masses.

As such, when news of Alexander's death reached her, she did as Alexander had commanded but, alas, nobody came to the banquet. And she asked, 'Why did the invitees not come?' And she was reminded that she had commanded that no one who had suffered tribulations might attend – but no human is spared tribulations and worry. To which she replied, 'O Alexander! How vigorous were your matters, and what analogy may be drawn by comparing your beginning to your epilogue! You wanted to comfort me, while you were completely consoled'.

68 | The Hebrew *Physiologus*

CHAPTER 10
ON PEACE

THEY COUNTED and concluded that there is no vessel (virtue) more capable of holding blessings than 'peace', such as the privilege of thought, spiritual naivety, an agreeable heart and a tranquil life – a companion and friend of 'justice'. The three kinds of 'peace' are: being at peace with yourself and your inciteful instincts (having inner peace); being at peace with God; and being at peace with fellow humans. As written (I Samuel 25: 6): 'Peace unto you, and peace unto your household, and peace unto all that is yours!' One can acquire this peace by learning the *Torah*, as said (Proverbs 3: 17): 'Her ways are pleasant ways and all her paths, peaceful.' R. Hillel said in tractate *Avot* (1: 12): 'Be a disciple of Aaron [the Priest], who loved and pursued peace, and loved all God's creations, by bringing them closer to the Torah.' In tractate *Shabbat* they said: 'The name of our blessed God is Peace,' as written in Judges (6: 24): 'and he [Gideon] called it [the altar] "God is peace".' We have determined that God's most essential blessing appears in Psalms (29: 11): 'May God grant strength to His People; God will bless His Nation with peace.'

Go out and see the virtue of peace in the creature that foreigners named *Castor* ('a beaver'); it is naturally aware that hunters pursue it for its testicles, which produce castoreum, known to have good medicinal properties. As such, whenever a *Castor* feels it is being pursued and has been cornered, unable to escape, it amputates its own testicles with its teeth and throws them aside, so that the hunters will take them, and it will be able to live on in peace.

Plato said that there is no wealth like peace and that one should always be at peace with the virtues and at war with one's faults in order to attain perfection.

In Roman books, it was written that there was a very important and brave soldier named Ippolito who, after the death of his father, was engaged for many days in a heavy war against a peer named Lystico, also a forceful and nice man. And from what Ippolito saw, he became very frightened, and his workers and servants were troubled by this heavy war. He arose in the middle of the night and went alone to his only enemy's fortress and called out: 'Open the gates for me, because I'm Ippolito and I came by myself.' The guards wondered and informed their master's inside. Once Lystico heard that his only enemy had come to him unarmed, he ordered the gate be opened. Ippolito ran to Lystico, hugging and kissing his enemy, and said:

> My dear and pleasant brother, I've come to ask for your pardon and forgiveness for all my iniquities, my sins against you, and I wholeheartedly pardon you for all your sins against me. I cry out to you for peace, because your reign over me is better than that of those who serve me.

When Lystico heard this, he also bowed like a reed, placing a rope around his head and kneeling before Ippolito, breaking out in tears. Both lamented and begged the other's forgiveness, saying: 'Brother, forgive me!' Thus, they made peace with each other, such as was not even seen between brothers from womb and birth, loyal and loving as they were all the rest of the days of their lives.

CHAPTER 11
ON ANGER

ACCORDING TO the researcher, 'anger' is confused thought along with blood circulating erratically around the heart, due to lust for vengeance. Similarly, the leading physician said that anger may be seen on the face of an angry person, whose body heats up and pulse quickens and gets stronger. Know that anger brings rage, since the enraged heart fills with turbid blood, that only later reverts to hate and clots. From these three – anger, rage and hate – come several other large transgressions and sins, including schisms, wars and competition, all contrary to peace, from which, as aforementioned, all goodness flows. Schisms occur when someone refuses or opposes another, rejecting whatever the other says or wants; this even happens among siblings, relatives and friends. Wars occur when people raise their hands against one another. Competition happens when people quarrel and say too many harsh words. Endless evils stem from anger,

Bears.
From chapter 11, 'On anger'.

besides its being an absolute sign of a lack of human reason. Solomon said (Ecclesiastes 7: 9): 'Don't let your spirit be quickly vexed, for vexation abides in the breasts of fools.' Also (Proverbs 29: 22): 'a hot-tempered man commits many offenses.' Our sages said that being angry is akin to idol worship [forbidden in Judaism]. In tractate *Pesahim* (66b), R. Shim'on b. Lakish said: 'Anyone who gets angry, if he is wise, his wisdom deserts him.' R. Mani [b. Patish] said: 'Whoever becomes angry, even if greatness has been apportioned to him from heaven, he is lowered from his greatness.' From this, we learn that especially leaders of others must avoid this vice (anger). As Solomon said (Proverbs 19: 11): 'A man shows intelligence by his forbearance; it is his glory when he overlooks an offence.' In other words, an intelligent man will not succumb to crime, nor will mishaps be caused by him.

We can compare the vice of anger to a bear that, by nature, eats honey; when it goes to get the honey from the beehive, the bees sting its eyes, so it runs after them to kill them. Should another one come and sting its face, it abandons the first chase, and pursues that one. All the while, its anger is growing inside, and even if there were a thousand bees, that bear would want to take revenge on them all. It has no self-control and will always run after the newest attacker in vain.

And Solomon said (Proverbs 27: 3): 'A stone has weight, sand is heavy, but a fool's vexation outweighs them both.' In the *Book of Ben Sira* it says: 'Anger burns like fire.' Seneca said that anger had no eyes, and that everything that is said and done out of anger cannot be just. Socrates said that the intellect sees the anger, but the anger does not see the intellect. And a sage said that, when dealing with someone angry, one must do three things: speak softly, be silent, and then depart. R. Shim'on b. El'azar already stated (in tractate *Avot* 4: 23): 'Do not try to appease your friend during his hour of anger.' It is also good to follow the (similar) recommendations of the *Aharonim* [rabbis and scholars from the sixteenth century on], based on three names in a biblical verse

(Genesis 25: 14): 'Mishma', Dumah and Massa"; (from the Hebrew roots meaning 'to listen', 'to be silent' and 'to go', discussed in tractate *Yoma* 23a: 3): 'Those who are insulted but do not insult others, who hear themselves being shamed but do not respond, act out of love for God'; and (Judges 5:31): '... love Him ... as the Sun, rising in its might!' And you must determine whether what is said to you as abuse and shaming is the truth or lies. If it is true, indeed your silence is preferable and required since you must refrain from shaming yourself further. If they spoke false ridicule and scorn (Psalms 85: 12): 'Truth springs up from the earth' and you will be revealed as being pure and clean. Therefore, whatever arouses your instincts to become angry, weigh all the sides (Ecclesiastes 11: 10): 'and banish anger from your heart and remove adversity from your flesh!'

It is written in a book that a gift was once brought to a great minister – several ceramic and glass dishes that were extremely beautiful, most lovely to behold. The minister saw them in a positive light, appreciating their craftsmanship. He applauded and thanked the one who had brought this gift to him, one worthy of his acceptance. Afterwards, the minister took them one by one and smashed them. Others asked him why he did that, and he replied:

> Because I, myself, know how great my inner anger and rage is. I sensed in my heart that if, today or tomorrow, one of my workers or servants would break them, I would rage at them and tread them with my wrath and trample them with my fury. Better I should break my own dishes now, than bring failure upon myself later.

CHAPTER 12
ON CHARITABLE ACTS

DOING 'ACTS OF loving kindness' means being merciful, benevolent and compassionate regarding the troubles of others. This virtue has two aspects – one is 'spiritual charity' and the other 'personal charity'. For example, acts of 'spiritual charity' might be forgiving someone his shame, or reproving a peer following a bad path (Proverbs 1: 4): 'endowing the simple with shrewdness' by providing sufficient counsel, consoling the bereaved, visiting the sick and praying for those suffering from afflictions, and for loved ones and those who hate you, living and dead. 'Personal charity' is sharing your food and drink with the hungry and thirsty, clothing the naked, welcoming visitors, redeeming captives and burying the dead. Essentially, one should be doing all these things out of a love of God, not for honour or glory. In this regard, Solomon (Proverbs 21: 21) said: 'He who strives to do good and kind deeds attains life, success and honour.' Indeed, 'loving kindness' is a virtue found, first and foremost in the Creator, as the poet said (Psalms 89: 15): 'Benevolence and truthfulness stand before You.' In *Bereshit Rabbah* (8: 13), R. Simlai said: 'We found that God blesses grooms and adorns brides, visits the sick and buries the dead; and he [Simlai] cited [biblical] verses attesting to all the above.' In light of Deuteronomy 13: 5: 'Follow none but the Lord your God', tractate *Sotah* (14a: 3–6) explains that just as God is merciful, so should we be. In the tractate *Sukkah* (49b: 11):

> Our Sages taught that acts of loving kindness are greater than charity in three ways: charitable acts involve only one's money, while acts of loving kindness may involve both one's personal services and money. Charity can be given only to the poor and the living, while acts of loving kindness may be done for the rich and the poor ... the living and the dead.

Partridges.
From chapter 24, 'On truthfulness'.

Above we taught two aspects – 'spiritual charity' and 'personal charity' – as it is written (Proverbs 11: 17): 'A kindly man benefits himself; a cruel man makes trouble for himself.'

The virtue of 'benevolence' also exists in red birds, Passerines, called *Pula* or *Pola* by foreigners. When the fledglings see that their parents are old, blind and unable to fly well – these fledglings toil and build a nest for their parents, bring them food and use their beaks to pluck out their parents' feathers, particularly those surrounding their eyes, that interfere with their eyesight, until new feathers grow out naturally and they even recover their eyesight. In regard to animals, this case relates more to honouring father and mother than to acts of loving kindness, in general, if they did not do all this only out of heartfelt mercy and benevolence.

We have already defined 'loving kindness'. As Solomon told us, all those who show benevolence will be shown benevolence (Proverbs 21: 13): 'Who stops his ears at the cry of the wretched, he too will call and not be answered.' Alexander said that the government of people can expand in three ways: by acquiring lovers (loving subjects), by showing mercy to others and forgiving enemies. More so, all the ruler's deeds should be done leniently, so he is considered 'pious', one who overlooks affronts (takes nothing personally). Pythagoras said that if your hand should hurt your eye, or your teeth, or your tongue, you would not seek vengeance against yourself – act similarly towards others. Plato stated that if every time someone sinned God punished that person, within a short time the world would return to chaos. Seneca said that you can imagine in your soul that you have already avenged yourself, then you can forgive your enemy. The world cannot exist without benevolence (Psalms 89: 3): 'For I have declared that a world of benevolence will establish the heavens.'

Benevolence for nations. It is written in Roman books that, during the reign of Alexander of Macedon, a wicked bully 'Corsair', caught one of the hatchlings in the ocean and brought it before him. Alexander asked the pirate why he sailed the seas to rob and commit acts of violence. The pirate replied: 'You've robbed the entire world, many nations and, in your wake, they call you their king; yet, I am but a single person in a single ship on the ocean, and they call me a robber. If you were anything like me, and they called you a robber, worse than me, what I run away from, you'd be chasing. My poverty and indigence led me to robbery, while your passion and covetousness led you to commit much worse robbery than mine. As long as you continue to succeed, you'll go on proudly, from one evil deed to the next. Had I had even a bit of tranquillity and goodness, I would have become better than you, never robbing again. Alexander appreciated the pirate's largesse and felt merciful towards him, understanding his needs that had driven him to do indecent deeds, and Alexander had mercy on him, and did not kill him, granting him mercy and appointing him to be one of his governors.

CHAPTER 13
ON CRUELTY

'CRUELTY' is a serious vice, contrary to benevolence and compassion. According to Aristotle, there are five types of 'cruelty': 1) a lack of mercy for others; 2) not providing necessary help that benefits another; 3) not forgiving affronts; 4) punishing others more than they deserve; and 5) to do bad things to another unjustifiably and without cause. The *Torah* says one should not be cruel even to one's enemies (Exodus 23: 5): 'When you see the ass of your enemy lying under its burden ... you must nevertheless raise it with him'; and (Proverbs 24: 17): 'I your enemy falls, do not exult; if he trips, let your heart not rejoice.' That is what distinguishes the righteous from the wicked, as written (Proverbs 12: 10): 'the compassion of the wicked is cruelty', since they are cruel by nature and use a show of compassion to promote praise. In tractate *Yevamot* (79a), it says of the Children of Israel: 'There are three distinguishing

Basilisk.
From chapter 13, 'On cruelty'.

marks of this nation: they are merciful, they are shamefaced, and they perform acts of kindness.'

The vice of cruelty is also found in a viper-like (reptilian creature) called *Basilisk* by the foreigners, that kills merely by its gaze and has not even a drop of compassion. When it cannot find a spot where it can strike a creature with its poison, it dries and burns the grasses and trees surrounding it with its shrieks and foul breath. The power of this vice is mostly utilised against the oppressed and the meek; thus, one must be especially wary of it.

In the *Book of Ben Sira* it says: 'Do not act like a lion in your home.' A sage said (Proverbs 30: 22): 'A slave who becomes king' is the cruellest of all. Another said: 'Do not torture the tortured, because he will abhor his life.' And Cassiodorus said: 'None are crueller than those who wish to get rich from the sweat of the poor.'

The ancients wrote that a woman named Medea desired a certain man, and followed him with her little brother, whom she murdered and chopped into pieces, that she threw down along her convoluted path, so that her father, who was pursuing her, would find the evidence of her inordinate cruelty, to shock and slow him down, while she escaped from him. After she had consummated her lust with that man and stayed with him a while, she bore his two sons. Then, when he left her, out of love for another woman, she murdered both sons and drank their blood to anger her husband. Afterwards, she wandered about the world, and her end is unknown.

CHAPTER 14
ON GENEROSITY

'GENEROSITY', in the opinion of the researcher, is a distinct form of giving, of an amount suited to the other (the recipient), someone worthy and needy, since giving to someone with no need is like adding a drop of water to the ocean. As Solomon said (Proverbs 22: 16): 'Giving gifts to the rich is pure loss.' And he who gives more than he can afford, departs from generosity, becoming a spendthrift, which is quite improper, spending what is inappropriate, lacking thriftiness and organisation, as any fool could tell him. As has been said, he who is wasteful should not waste more than a fifth. Such a one would sink rapidly from being a spendthrift to being impoverished, which is why one needs self-restraint to distinguish between generosity and spendthriftiness. The *Torah* contains much praise of generosity, as written (Exodus 35: 10): 'Let all the generous of heart come and do as God commands'; and (Isa. 32: 8): 'And the generous advises generosity'; and (Psalms 47:10): 'The generous among the nations were gathered with Abraham's God.' In tractate *Gittin* 7: 1: R. Yishma'el said that: 'anyone who shaves off some of his assets and gives it to charity is saved from the judgement of Hell.' There is a parable about two ewes crossing a stream, one that had been sheared and the other that had not; the sheared sheep made it across, while the unsheared sheep did not.

The virtue of 'generosity' may be seen in the eagle, the most generous of all the birds, since it is told about the eagle that, even when it is very hungry, it will leave half its food for the birds nearby while it is eating; thus, it flies on little sustenance against other predators trying to eat it – those after which other birds will not follow to eat scraps.

Solomon says in his book, Proverbs (Ecclesiastes 11: 1): 'Send your bread forth upon the waters; for after many days you will find

Wild ass.
From chapter 36, 'On abstinence'.

it.' Also (Proverbs 18: 16): 'A man's gift eases his way and gives him access to the great.' You should use your money to benefit your loved ones, rather than burying it in the earth or spending it on pleasures. Alexander said you should give to others, and they will give to you. And if you want to quickly improve on your gift, then give two gifts in rapid succession.

This is the tale about Naḥum Ish Gamzu [a first-century sage], told by the sages in tractate *Ta'anit* (21a: 9–10). He had lost the use of both his hands and both his feet, was blind in both eyes, and his entire body was covered by boils. When he was asked, 'Why has this befallen you?', he told them:

> My sons, I caused this to myself. Once, when I was walking to the home of my father-in-law, with three donkey's worth of food, one of drink, and another with various sweets. A poor man came up to me and stood near me in the road, and said: 'Rabbi, provide for me.' I told him: 'Wait until I unload the donkey.' But before I managed to unload the donkey, he died. I went and threw myself

down upon him and said: 'May my eyes that did not have mercy on your eyes lose their sight; may my hands that showed no mercy.'

Indeed, do not be lax when giving to a pauper, for that is the cause of this adversity.

Tacitus said that, when indicated, you should be generous with your money and not complain, and give your gift affably, because gentle words are better than a gift. As stated in tractate *Bava Batra* (9: 2), R. Yitzḥak says: 'Anyone who gives a *peruta* ['a penny'] to a poor person receives six blessings, and whoever consoles him with words of comfort and encouragement receives eleven blessings.' Seneca said that it is more appropriate to observe the face and good will of the giver than the hand of the receiver, and that nothing costs more than what is attained by means of entreaties, and that the giver should remain silent, since the gift says it all. He who requests charity with dread, teaches the one asked to refuse the request, and it is written that when the master is generous, the slaves cannot be stingy, for they must do as their master's wills. The Lord, our God, is generous; why then would we, his servants, be misers.

It is written in a book that a poor tramp came before the King, Alexander of Macedon, and requested a penny of charity from him. The king offered the tramp a large city. And the poor man said: 'Ahhh, my Lord King! Such a large city does not befit me.' To which Alexander responded: 'Ahhh, brother! But the miniscule gift for which you asked also does not befit you; therefore, I don't know what you do deserve to get, only what is appropriate for me to give.' King Antigonus did the opposite to find a reason to refuse a request by replying with a syllogism: 'It is not appropriate for someone as small as you to make such a large request.'

CHAPTER 15
ON GREED

'GREED' (also known as 'avarice' or 'miserliness') is the opposite of 'generosity'. In Tullio's opinion, this vice promotes malice and covetousness, seeking to purchase and acquire great wealth, in an honest or fickle manner. A miser would rather watch his own acquired assets lost or rotting, than give them to others. 'Greed' is far worse than 'spendthriftiness', because 'spendthriftiness' is more like 'generosity', since its main principle is giving, while 'greed' is basically prevention (amassing wealth only for oneself). While a spendthrift can more easily distance himself from spendthriftiness and return to reasonable moderation, it is much harder for a miser to start giving. A sage said that the miser keeps for himself what he ought to be spending and only spends what is fit to keep. Another said that every purpose has its limit, except

Toad.
From chapter 15, 'On greed'.

82 | The Hebrew *Physiologus*

for greed, that has neither limit nor purpose. Our sages said (*Kohelet Rabbah* 1: 13): 'No one leaves this world with half their passion in hand.' Another sage said that all the improper vices grow old in the world, except for greed, which renews itself and returns every day.

And we can compare the miser ('greed') to what the foreigners call *Rospo* ('a toad'), that lives on dirt and also leaves it behind, lest it be lacking, so it never eats enough to be satiated.

Solomon said (Ecclesiastes 6: 1–2):

> There is an evil I have observed under the Sun, and a grave one it is for man, that God sometimes grants a man riches, property, and respect, so that he does not want for anything his appetite may crave, but God does not permit him to enjoy it; instead, a stranger will enjoy it.

Such a man will say: 'I hate all the work I do under the Sun, leaving everything behind for another man.' Pythagoras said that it is like the donkey's saddlecloth, that benefits the rider, but harms the donkey, thus greed harms he who has it, benefitting his heirs. Seneca said that it is appropriate to command the money, but not to serve it. Once the love of money has grown, the connection with people will be reduced. Furthermore, there are those among them (misers) whom you will not enjoy, preferring their deaths, because they are fools and misers – since it is better to respect someone penniless than to respect the money and not the people. Priscian said that as long as it rains when the ground is hard, so the miser will increase his greed, and will not compassionately seed the ground to reap twofold, rather he will be disinclined to give anything to another, because he has the invisible advantage. However, the money does not belong to the miser, the miser belongs to the money. Another said that one should call a miser an 'idol worshipper', for he worships idols of silver and gold, and the miser knows no other god than money. As it is written in the *Torah* (Exodus 20: 20): 'You shall not make any gods of silver, nor shall you make for yourselves any gods of gold.' And Seneca wondered what amassing more silver and gold gives a miser; money was given for spending, God did not want these treasures to remain buried in the quarry. R. Ibn Gabirol wrote that the cure for this vice is for the miser to habituate himself to volunteer on behalf of relatives, until he would gradually do so with those more distant and become accustomed to generosity.

In books, we read about an extremely greedy man, who collected a countless amount of silver, gold and money. When he got ill and it was his time to die, he commanded that his fountains full of gold items and silver coins be brought before him, so he might touch them, saying: 'Help me, help me! Protect me, protect me! Cure me from my ailment!' But when he saw that it did no good, he summoned his sons and told them:

> My sons, you are aware of all the hardship I took upon myself, to amass all this; however, even my little finger got no joy from these objects, and now, in my time of need, they did not save me. Therefore, I order you to spend them generously on appropriate things. For even if I lived a thousand years, I could not have altered my habits, being steeped in this evil vice. So now, you use what I served all the days of my life.

CHAPTER 16
ON ADMONITION

ACCORDING TO the opinion of our sages, 'admonition' is an outcome of love, when someone suitably admonishes a friend for saying or doing something improper. An individual is too close to himself and may not see his own responsibility for his deeds, as such, someone else who loves him is needed to admonish and chastise him. Needless to say, in regard to all the youths and children in the entire world, whose years and experiences are few, that they need this. 'If folly settles in the heart of a lad, the rod of discipline will remove it' (Proverbs 22: 15). There is a horsewhip, a bit for the mule, and a rod for the backs of fools. 'Discipline your son while there is still hope, and do not set your soul on his destruction' (Proverbs 19: 18). 'He who reproves a man will, in the end, find more favour than he who flatters him' (Proverbs 28: 23), said Solomon. And the *Torah* states that we must perform commandments (Leviticus 19: 17): 'Reprove your kinsman, but incur no guilt because of him,' for if your do not admonish him, you will also bear his iniquity and punishment. As discussed in tractate *Berakhot* (31a: 28; that also cites I Samuel 1: 14): 'How long will you make a drunken spectacle of yourself?' Thus, when one observes something indecent in a friend, one is obliged to admonish him. Our sages often say that whenever it is possible to admonish those in your home, but you did not do so, they will find you remiss, and in your city, and in the world. Show no bias towards anyone anywhere who has blasphemed against God. And should you see someone transgressing, take action if it is in your power to prevent it by means of talk or the use of force. Of course, the admonisher must take the utmost care to stay safe and must first be untainted by personal sin and inappropriate vices – actually practising what he wishes to teach others by means of force or words, so it not be said of him what R. Tarfon said in tractate *'Arakhin* (16b):

I would be surprised if there is anyone in this generation who can receive rebuke. Why? Because if the one rebuking says to him: 'Remove the splinter from between your eyes', i.e., rid yourself of a minor infraction, the other says to him: 'Remove the beam from between your eyes', meaning, you have committed far more severe sins.

Zephaniah the Prophet has already commented on this (Zephaniah 2: 1): 'Gather together, gather, O nation without shame', because the words preached by men who practise them are fine. Nonetheless, blessed is the person who obeys his teachers, educators and those who admonish him, regardless of who he is, and who pays attention to their words and not to the one who said (Proverbs 12: 1): 'He who loves discipline loves knowledge; he who spurns reproof is a brutish man.' Tractate 'Arakhin (16b) also states that R. Yoḥanan b. Nuri attested that R. 'Akiva was lashed (i.e., punished) many times on his account, because R. Yoḥanan complained about R. 'Akiva to Rabban Gamliel, but that,

Mule.
From chapter 16, 'On admonition'.

86 | The Hebrew *Physiologus*

nonetheless, R. 'Akiva continued to love him for having observed the saying (Proverbs 9: 8): 'Do not rebuke a scoffer, for he will hate you; reprove a wise man, and he will love you.'

Go out and learn! This virtue ('admonition') is found in the wolf, of which it is said that, when it goes to prey near any house or residence, if the ground is not level and it loses its footing when walking, so that the people sense its presence, it must turn back and flee for its life. Later, it puts that foot between its teeth and bites it – to torment and chastise it regarding the bad it caused that it might learn to fear the next time, to walk a straight, as it wanted. It seems, from this, that as long the sinner is ourselves, our flesh and blood, our loved ones, it is all the more appropriate that we provide admonition, as written (Proverbs 27: 5–6): 'Open reproof is better than concealed love. Wounds by a loved one are long lasting; the kisses of an enemy are profuse.' Diogenes said that someone who wishes to befriend another should admonish him privately, because the use of soft language adds love; while he who chastises another using harsh words will acquire only hatred. Cato said that if the person you chastised continues to sin often, you must continue your frequent reproofs. Plato said to beware tormenting your friend in public when he is angry. And our devout prophets wrote, to tell the generations, that one must not refrain from admonishing members of their generation, peers and those who stray, even if they go on being shameful and causing harm, because that was what others did.

See a *midrash* on the Prophet Isaiah, taken from *Tanna Devei Eliyahu Rabbah* (Chapter 16):

> Once I was sitting in the Great Study Hall in Jerusalem and a student came and asked me, like a son asking his father: 'How is Isaiah different from all the other Prophets, who foresaw all the good things and consolations in Israel?' I said to him: 'My son, because he accepted heaven's yoke with joy, as written [Isaiah 6: 8–9]: 'Then I heard the voice of the Lord ...'Go speak [to the People].'

And it was interpreted that Isaiah was granted this despite the fact that he had said that nobody would listen to him and respect him (Isaiah 6: 10): 'Dull that people's mind.' Yet, Isaiah did not refrain from going out and admonishing them joyfully. In the end, he gave his life (was martyred) out of love for the sanctity of God, as told in a *midrash* (in tractate *Yevamot* 49b), that Manasseh (King of Israel) sent men after him to kill him. And Isaiah uttered a divine name and was swallowed within a cedar tree. Manasseh's servants brought back that cedar tree and sawed through it to kill him. When the saw reached his mouth, Isaiah died.

As Isaiah said in his book (Isaiah 50: 6): 'I offered my back to the floggers, and my cheeks to those who tore out my hair; I did not hide my face.' Indeed, even when they tortured him on the wheel, threw him in a pit, hit and wounded him, he said (Jeremiah 11: 19): 'I was like a docile lamb led to the slaughter.' And (Jeremiah 15: 10): 'I have not lent, and I have not borrowed; yet everyone curses me.' How many prophets and pious men in each generation did not refrain when facing the shaming and beatings incurred when admonishing their friends, and how great is the privilege of someone who brings people back from their bad ways; tractate *Avot* (5: 20): 'because the righteousness of the multitudes depends on Him' and God's justice is eternal.

88 | The Hebrew *Physiologus*

CHAPTER 17
ON FLATTERY

THE FLATTERER stands in direct opposition to the admonisher, speaking words of magnificence and praise to someone or about that person's deeds, whether true or false, in order to gain some benefit from that person, like reeling in a whale. But they also say that perhaps he (the flatterer) is speaking pleasantly, to placate and please others, rather than attempting to take something from them; that may be termed 'wisdom', because the sages said (in tractate *Ketubot* 17a): 'A person's disposition should always be empathetic with Mankind.'

The community of flatterers is similar to the Siren, a creature in the ocean, the top part of which resembles a woman, the bottom part a fish, and that dwells among dangerous boulders mid-ocean. Whenever a ship passes nearby, the Siren begins to sing in a very alluring voice, until she causes all the sailors to fall asleep, even the captains and leaders. Afterwards, she boards the ship, kills and eats them all.

Solomon said (Proverbs 11: 9): 'The words of the flatterer destroy his friend but, by their knowledge, the righteous are saved.' And Elihu said (Job 36: 13): 'And sycophants become enraged; they do not cry for help when He binds them.' And Job (27: 8) said: 'For what hope has the flatterer when he is cut down, when God takes away his life?'

And it is written (Proverbs 24: 24): 'He who says to the wicked, "You are righteous" shall be cursed by nations.' R. Eli'ezer ('the Great,' b. Hurkanus) often spoke ill of this vice, saying that anyone full of flattery will be cursed, even by passers-by. In tractate *Sotah* (7: 8), a story is told about King (Herod) Agrippa, who stood and read the *Torah* portion aloud to the congregation. When he reached the verse (Deuteronomy 17: 15), 'You must be sure to set a king over yourself, one of your own people;

you must not set a foreigner over you, who is not from among your brethren', tears flowed from his eyes. He was told: 'Have no fear, King Agrippa – you are our brother.' As R. Nathan said: 'At that very hour, the enemies of Israel, a generation of sycophants, were found guilty – since they had flattered Agrippa.' This teaches you that it is even forbidden to flatter the king that one is obliged to fear and respect – flattering is forbidden. In truth, especially those who flatter kings and national advisers, their iniquities are unbearable, because when they misguide the rulers and leaders, they mislead the masses, as well; and they will pay for it in the future.

Tullio said that we should be well-liked by everyone, be affable with everybody, but must not deal in flattery, nor make too many friends. Averroes said that beneath the flatterer's honey lays wormwood and poison. Aesop said that pleasant words may lead to bad deeds. Even dogs always love to find a bone to eat. And the bee will always love a blooming plant. Cato said we should remember, whenever someone praises us, to be a judge, and not to believe in others more than in yourself. Plato said, never trust someone who praises you more than what is befitting you, because he will also condemn you, more than you deserve; because the scorpion incites with its mouth but strikes with its tail. Socrates said that as the grass covers the land, the flatterer will hide his defects.

And Aesop told a parable about the vice of 'flattery'. Once a fox saw a raven with a piece of cheese in its beak. The fox thought how it might snatch that cheese, so it began to praise and glorify the raven. The fox said: 'Brother, there's no more beautiful bird or fowl than you. Would that sound of your birdsong be as beautiful as your body! For none are like you, nor equal to you in all the land and above it.' When the raven heard all these praises about himself, he wanted to make his voice heard in song, so he opened his mouth to sing – the cheese fell out and the fox took it. And the fox said: 'The acclaim is for you and the cheese is mine.' Thus, the raven was left in shame and disgrace.

CHAPTER 18
ON DILIGENCE

'DILIGENCE,' 'prudence' and 'industriousness' reflect the intelligence and knowledge to foresee the future and the ability to state the outcomes at the beginnings of all one's dealings. R. Ibn Gabirol wrote that 'diligence' is, by nature, the red bile (symbolic of strength and hope), more easily observed when the soul is free of the indecent vices, and no worry confuses this virtue, and it suits the person who will apply 'prudence' in all his dealings – seeking wisdom, faith and his basic needs.

Look and understand the virtue of 'diligence' in the ant, that rushes on summer days to capture and store prey for its sustenance in the autumn season, preparing in the present for the future, when it might not find what it seeks. To that end, the ant sets out to survey the area, and carries the wheat, and stores it away as helpful (reserved) food during winter days. About the ant Solomon said (Proverbs 6: 6): 'Lazybones, go to the ant; study its ways and learn.' Prepare your sustenance in the summer.

Solomon said (Proverbs 4: 4): 'diligent hands enrich.' He also said (Ecclesiastes 2: 4): 'A wise man has eyes in his head.' And R. Shim'on said in tractate *Avot* (2: 9): 'someone with foresight.' Tullio said that it is unbecoming of a wise man to say, 'I had no idea such a thing could happen to me', because if he was truly wise, he would not fear, rather hope, and he would not sigh, rather think. Perseus said that man, like a boat, can sink, and several others will sink with it. Aristotle said that a fool thinks that luck causes good and evil, though wisdom provides goodness, while foolishness, evil; appropriate deeds attest to honest forethought. Branchus said that the key to real security is considerable forethought, and that he who rarely thinks will make many errors. [Note that the Hebrew translation reads 'Braco', while in the earlier Italian *Fior di Virtù* (Chapter 19), this name appears as 'Branchus'.]

Magpies.
From chapter 7, 'On envy'.

Alexander said that night was made for thinking; and day for deeds. Seneca said that it is easier to face things at the onset than at the conclusion, just as fresh grass is soft and easier to pull out than fixed underground roots, which are hard to weed. Cato said that the possibility to survive is always important, because one can usually cure a disease recognised early. Solomon said (Proverbs 11: 14): 'victory follows much [good] advice.' Aristotle said that he used to procrastinate and accept advice as a last resort, though now he quickly accepts present counsel. Theophrastus said that nothing good happens without agility. While another said that running water never becomes poisonous. And Plato said that wisdom without experience and agility is good for nothing.

The Romans wrote in their books that once, when the Caesar was riding his horse in a dense forest, there, he found a philosopher and called out to him but got no reply. So, the Caesar called out to him a second time, and again got no reply. When the Caesar saw this, he approached the philosopher and asked him what he was doing in the forest. The philosopher responded: 'I'm learning wisdom.' 'If so,' said the Caesar, 'learn from it also for me.' So, the philosopher took a piece of paper and wrote on it: 'Whatever you agree to do, first think how you will go on from there.' And he gave that note to the Caesar, who returned to Rome and placed that note at the entrance to his palace. In those days, some of the king's great ministers wished to assassinate the Caesar. And they swore to pay gold and many pearls to the Caesar's royal barber if he would slit the Caesar's throat while shaving his beard. And the barber agreed, as long as they would save him from being put to death – so they promised. Then, on the day that the barber went to shave the Caesar, in order to slit his throat, as the conspirators had agreed among themselves, but when the barber reached the king's gate, he lifted his eyes and saw the philosopher's epigram and read the words: 'Whatever you agree to do, first think how you will go on from there.' These words pierced his heart and scared him very much, because he thought it was an epigram from the king, written after hearing the advice (of his advisers); so, he immediately went and fell to his knees before the king, crying, pleading for forgiveness, and revealing the entire conspiracy plot, of which the Caesar knew nothing. When the Caesar heard about this, he had his ministers brought before him and put them to death; he sent the barber home. Then, the Caesar summoned the philosopher who had given him the epigram and kept him at his side from then on, out of love and great respect.

CHAPTER 19
ON FOOLISHNESS

'FOOLISHNESS' is a vice contrary to 'diligence', having various types, since there are certainly more fools in the world than wise men, although it is written of wise men (Ecclesiastes 10: 1): 'a little folly outweighs massive wisdom.' Indeed, there are common and absolute fools, like vagrants who remain outside human society or those who temporarily lose their minds, for a month or a year, during which time they resemble the aforementioned fools. Some among them seem to be intelligent, but occasionally their opinions change for certain periods, called 'lunatics' by foreigners. There are others who become fools when overwhelmed by black bile (i.e., melancholy) and nervousness, rendering them entirely mindless. And all these engendered countless more types. There are also fools lacking in sufficient intelligence and those having four distinct aspects: 1) he who barely considers his actions and fills his heart with desire, without checking if it is good or bad; 2) he who is unable to see what is coming his way and what each day may bring; 3) an impetuous person who acts in haste, without forethought or seeking counsel; and 4) someone who refuses to behave decently, suitably, out of overwhelming laziness, that prevents him from beginning to do so.

We can relate 'foolishness' to a species of wild bull, Aurochs [now extinct], that naturally hated the colour red (as other species of wild bulls still do today). As such, when hunters want to capture a wild bull, they wear red clothing and walk where it walks and can see them. Right away, and without any preparation and forethought, the ill-tempered and enraged bull runs, chasing after them, while they flee and hide behind a predetermined tree, marked by them in advance. The bull charges them so hastily, intending to butt the hunters, that it rams into the tree, getting its horns deeply stuck in the tree, so much so that it cannot get free. Then, the hunters go to it and kill it.

Fox. From chapter 23, 'On dishonesty and deceit'.

Thus, Solomon spoke pejoratively and with contempt about fools in Proverbs (1: 32): 'The frivolity of simpletons will kill them; and the complacency of dullards will destroy them'; and (Proverbs 13: 20): 'he who consorts with fools comes to grief.' Also (Proverbs 14: 7): 'Keep your distance from a fool; the mouth of a fool is ruinous to himself and to many.' And our sages said in tractate *Berakhot* that 'knowledge' is great when situated between two divine names (as in I Samuel 2: 3): 'for the Lord is an all-knowing God.' They also said that anyone (*Leviticus Rabbah* 1: 15): 'lacking knowledge is no better than a carcass.' Diogenes said that there is no greater wealth than knowledge, and there is no shortage of fools. Ptolemy stated that no one died after being revived by wisdom and nobody became impoverished once having acquired knowledge.

Writers have told us that Alexander of Macedon and Aristotle used to stroll together in Macedonia with servants walking before them and announcing: 'Make way for King Alexander!' Once, a fool was sitting on a rock in the middle of the path and did not wish to get up. One of the eunuchs tried to fend him off, remove him from there. Aristotle told the eunuch, 'Do not remove a rock from atop a rock, because a fool is not really human.'

CHAPTER 20
ON JUSTICE AND JUDGEMENT

'JUSTICE' MEANS giving each individual exactly what that person deserves, and no more. Three conditions must be fulfilled to provide quick and just 'judgement': 1) he (the judge) must have the (legal) power and (governmental) authority to do so; 2) he must know and have mastered the (issue) he wishes to judge; and 3) he must truly want to make a just and honest ruling.

Look to what is right and see 'justice' and 'judgement' in 'the king of the bees' (Psalms 112: 5): 'who conducts his affairs with equity.' Since some of the bees are tasked with gathering the nectar from the flowers for making the honey, while the work of the others is to repair and complete the honeycomb, and others are commanded to accompany (guard) the king, and the rest to serve as an army to protect the hive. In nature, they fight a great battle, each one wanting to take the honey from another, yet not a single bee ever leaves the hive before its king, and all greatly respect him. Proverbs (22: 6): 'Train a lad in the way he ought to go; he will not swerve from it even in old age'; Proverbs (31: 29): 'Many women have succeeded greatly' and will carry the king bee wherever he wills. And all the other bees have stings in their tails, except for the king, and some of these king bees are black, while others are bigger and ruddier than the rest.

Solomon said in his book of wisdom that you should not ask to be a judge if you cannot bear to chastise your friends, and that the judges in the Land of Israel must love jurisprudence. Hermetes said that one should never punish a person without first letting him state his claims, and do not overly delay punishment, lest justice be delayed. Seneca said that he who cannot command himself should not command others. Tullio said that complete justice cannot exist if even one of its steps is missing. A sage said that five things can lose a trial: love, envy, supplication, fear and bribery. Socrates said that the mayors of cities should beware the company of the wicked, for all the evil found in a city is ascribed to its mayor. Plato said, never advise someone who is more able than you, because he may use your advice to your detriment. And what is more pleasant than the brief words of the Prophet Isaiah (Isaiah 32: 1): 'Indeed, a king shall reign with justice.'

Truly, there are God's judges on Earth (those who uphold His just laws) (Deuteronomy 32: 4): 'all His ways are just.' We found it written that there was once a long-devout, pious recluse subject to many bad, chronic ailments, from which he could not recover. When he began to challenge God and spoke harshly in his prayers, an angel of God appeared before him and said to him: 'Come with me! For God has commanded me to show you the secrets and mysteries of His ways.' So, he went with the angel and they arrived at a house that had a box full of golden coins, that the angel took and left before the entrance of another home. Later, the angel walked the recluse over to another home, where he killed a baby laying in its crib.

Bees.
From chapter 20, 'On justice and judgement'.

When the recluse saw those things, he wanted to get away from him, thinking that he was a demon or some total evildoer. Indeed, the angel commanded him:

Stand where you are, and I will teach you understanding. Regarding all the money I took, there was just cause, because the owner had sold all his assets to accumulate gold coins, so he might hire an assassin to kill another man who long hated him. Had that man been murdered, all the townsfolk would have groaned, since the murder victim was an honest man. As such, I removed the obstacle [defused that option], so the owner might repent his evil thoughts [and recant his intentions]. I, then, placed them in another doorway, because the man of the house had lost his ship at sea with all his possessions and, in his great distress and anger, he wanted to strangle himself, but now he'd find the money, be consoled, live, and not die.

I killed that baby because, before it was born, its father had been a simple, honest, God-fearing man, but once the baby was born, he turned into a wicked person, robbing, and doing wrong; for the sins of their fathers, small sons die [cf. Exodus 20:5], so that the baby's father would return from his evil path. You, too, should not be puzzled by all your sufferings, because God sees and knows all about you. Perhaps, if we didn't see you as you are, if you weren't a pious recluse, and you, yourself, believed that there is no good or evil coming down from above, but rather [divine] justice, not suspecting God of imposing an unjust punishment [cf. tractate *Berakhot* 5b: 17], of choosing a lesser evil – however, people who didn't know and didn't honour God – even they would be astonished and consider it miraculous.

When the angel finished speaking these words to him, it disappeared, after which the recluse went to confirm the truth of those words and found them all to be undeniably true; thus, the recluse returned to his right mind and to the pursuit of justice and mercy, as before.

98 | The Hebrew *Physiologus*

CHAPTER 21
ON WRONGDOING AND LAWLESSNESS

'WRONGDOING', 'injustice' and 'lawlessness' are the opposites of 'justice' and 'judgement', which delay straightness and function illegally. They have different aspects: 1) spills innocent blood; 2) is spiteful of others; 3) uses brute force and coercion on others; 4) harms others physically or financially; 5) steals secretly; 6) commits violent robberies; or 7) commits perjury, framing the innocent or swearing that the guilty is innocent. Indeed, that was the sin of the generation of the Great Flood, as written (Genesis 6: 11): 'The Earth became corrupt before God; the Earth was filled with lawlessness.' Even though there were idolators, committers of incest, and those who shed (innocent) blood among them, and all the rest of the world's sins, their verdict was not sealed until they committed robbery and lawlessness.

We can associate this bad vice with the Devil, who never lodges any justice in the world, and all whose intentions are to commit evil deeds each day, to worsen the lives of his worshippers, and to repay goodness with badness. As the *Torah* repeatedly states (Deuteronomy 25: 16): 'For all wrongdoers are abhorrent to the Lord your God.' And David said (Psalms 37: 1): 'do not be incensed by wrongdoers.' And he also said (Psalms 125: 3): 'that the righteous not set their hand to wrongdoing.' In the *Jerusalem Talmud*, tractate *Peah* (7: 10) it states: 'Whosoever does not allow the poor to gather the gleanings [left in the field after the harvest] or allows only one specific [poor person] and not another to do so – indeed, this is robbery.' It is also said (Proverbs 23: 10): 'Do not move ancient boundaries.' In the *Book of Ben Sira* it says that if you judge others, others will judge you. Solomon said Ecclesiastes 10: 8): 'He who digs a pit will fall into it; he who breaches a stone fence will be bitten by a snake.' And one sage said that nothing good can succeed that comes

Aurochs.
From chapter 19, *'On foolishness'*.

from something bad; while another said that anyone who harms another, will also come to harm, and will not know from where it came.

We found it written that the Devil agreed to take a wife to bear daughters for him, so he might bring his sons-in-law to his home in Hell. As such, he chose Wrongdoing to be his wife and she bore him seven daughters. These are the names of his daughters, whom he gave in marriage to their husbands: 1) the eldest was named Pride and she was given to the ministers; 2) Greed was betrothed to the public masses; 3) Falsehood, to the villagers and peasant farmers; 4) Envy, to the tradesmen; 5) Flattery, to the hypocrites and pseudo-pious; and 6) Vanity, to the women; while 7) Lewdness, the Devil did not want to give in marriage, because he let her become a prostitute across the land so, like now, she might cause the death of a great nation – all these were birthed by Wrongdoing, who never foamed at the mouth.

CHAPTER 22
ON LOYALTY

'LOYALTY' or 'trustworthiness' is seeing the truth as it is in all its interactions with the people, whether a master or a superior, an equal or a subordinate. The quality of this virtue is such that God, Lord of all the prophets, spoke it in praise of Moses, the Prophet, as written (Numbers 12: 7): 'Not so with my servant Moses; he is trusted throughout my household.'

This virtue ('loyalty') is found in birds called cranes (or *Grus* by foreigners) that have a king that they serve more loyally than all the other living creatures. As such, when they want to sleep at night, they position their king in the centre, surrounding him, while two or three cranes stand guard. And so that sleep will not overcome these guards, they always keep one leg up in the air and the other on the ground, while the raised foot grasps a stone. Should they begin to fall asleep, the rock falls and they feel it and awaken. All this they do to loyally serve their king.

Phoenix.
From chapter 30, 'On strength and fortitude'.

One should be trustworthy in all one's dealings and always do everything loyally and honestly. Solomon said (Proverbs 20: 6): 'He calls many a man his loyal friend, but who can find a faithful man?' In tractate *Shabbat* (31a: 11) our sages instructed us that people must first be inculcated with this virtue (loyalty). Rava said: '[After dying], when a person is brought to judgement for the life he lived [in this world], they ask him: "Did you conduct business faithfully?"' He also said (tractate *Shabbat* 119b: 11): 'Jerusalem was destroyed only because there were no more trustworthy people there.' As stated in (Jeremiah 5: 1): 'Roam the streets of Jerusalem, search its squares, look about and take note. You will not find a man; there is none who acts justly, who seeks integrity, that I should pardon her [Jerusalem].' Seneca said that he who loses his trustworthiness has nothing left to lose. Aristotle said that one should not withhold one's loyalty with anyone, because the lack of trust is a vice of prostitutes and wrongdoers. Socrates said you should be loyal to those who believe in you and avoid sinning. Juvenal said that all the things in the world are either condemned or praised by someone, but loyalty is praised by everyone the world over. Another said by three things a person can rise to greatness: by being loyal; by speaking truth; and by avoiding vile thoughts.

It is written in Roman books that during the Carthaginian (Punic) wars against Rome, Roman General Marcus Regulus was captured and sent to Rome in an attempt to exchange prisoners of war, to release Carthaginians being held in Rome. When the Roman Senate had met to discuss that plan, Regulus had rejected it, stating that it was a bad plan for the Romans, because those Roman captives in Carthage were contemptible people, mostly elderly, unable to take any captives in battle, while the Carthaginian captives being held in Rome were heroic, the best, strong young men. Therefore, they accepted his words and refused to make the prisoner exchange. Marcus Regulus, as a man of his word, returned to Carthage, showing his loyalty both to his own nation and to the captors.

102 | The Hebrew *Physiologus*

CHAPTER 23
ON DISHONESTY AND DECEIT

'DISHONESTY' is the opposite of 'trustworthiness'; it is saying or doing something to deceive or cheat someone by being two-faced and altering one's visage to suit each deceptive scam. All the flatterers, and you, should know that thinking ill of others and scepticism are based in malevolent thoughts. 'Deceit' is also contrary to 'trustworthiness', as the Prophet said (Isaiah 7: 9): 'If you do not believe, you will not be believed.' A sage said that this vice stems from four things: 1) wicked people believe that everyone is wicked like them; 2) they were taught it; 3) out of hatred for the person about whom he is thinking; and 4) having had several such experiences. The researcher said that old people are frequently apprehensive due to their many lifelong experiences. Recognise the distinction between 'apprehension' and 'envy', because 'envy' comes from love.

This improper vice ('deceit') may be observed in the fox. When it does not find what it wants to eat, it throws itself on the ground, laying prostrate, as though dead. Those carrion-eating birds, that believe it is dead, will surround it, observing it, even climbing on it, and once the fox senses that they are standing near him unguardedly, the fox pounces and eats as many as he can.

David said (Psalms 12: 4): 'May the Lord cut off all flattering lips', meaning lips that impart deceitful words to attain devious ends. Solomon said (Proverbs 30: 8): 'Keep empty and false words far from me.' Our sages forbade us to even speak fraudulent words, as written in tractate *Bava Metsi'a*, based on the verse (Leviticus 25: 17): 'Do not wrong one another, but fear your God, for I, the Lord, am your God.' And in tractate *Ḥullin*, they said that it is forbidden to deceive people, even if they are not of your religion, and our sages also said that you should not convince someone to eat with you if it is forbidden for him to do so. Seneca said that a deceitful man

Sparrows.
From chapter 31, 'On fickleness'.

pretends not to feel shame, so he can wreak stronger vengeance. Another said that many times a wolf will cover itself in sheepskin. Plato admitted that he regretted two things – when the wealthy are disgraced and when the fool deceives the wise man. Solomon, in his book of wisdom, wrote that in the case of a deceitful man, his death is better than his life, because if he tries to be loyal, no one will believe him, and everyone will chase him away. Alexander said that you should not suspect someone in whom you placed your trust without just cause, because no good will come of it. Another said you should be concerned when you trust two who are enemies. Socrates said that all who love are also fearful, but many are fearful, though loveless. Our sages taught us that every person is worthy of respect but suspect. In tractate Hullin (Chpter 7), it says that one may not offer to sell someone leather sandals without informing him of the source of the leather. Similarly, as in the story about a man who sent his friend as cask full of wine instead of oil. When that man had guests and discovered that he had been deceived, he choked himself to death, out of shame.

CHAPTER 24
ON TRUTHFULNESS

THE 'TRUTH' is known to express things as really experienced, not falsely, both in regard to numerous things and in response to a single thing, as attestation and regarding everything – although the virtue of 'truthfulness' or 'honesty' is more precise among the pious, interpreted as in the verse (Psalms 15: 2): 'in his heart acknowledges the truth.' As in the case of R. Safra, who had determined to sell his *ḥameyts* [leavened foods forbidden during Passover] for five *dinars* [to non-Jews before the festival], but they offered him twenty *dinars*, which he rejected, even though he had not stated what he had in mind, thus, remaining true to himself.

A parable on the virtue of 'honesty' talks about the offspring of what the foreigners call *Pirnitso* ('a partridge'); each time she lays her eggs, another broody *Pirnitso* comes and takes them to her nest and sits on them, but once they hatch, these hatchlings naturally recognise the voice of their real birth mother and immediately go back to her. This is, indeed, the truth, that is revealed in the end, as written (Psalms 85: 12): 'Truth springs up from the earth.'

Doves. *From chapter* 38, 'On modesty'.

David said (Psalms 51: 8): 'Indeed, you desire truth'; while his son Solomon said (Proverbs 12: 19): 'Truthful speech abides forever'; and (Proverbs 3:3): 'May benevolence and truth never leave you.' In tractate *Shabbat* (55a: 2), R. Ḥanina said: 'The seal of the Holy One, Blessed be He, is truth' – the God of truth desires only honest people, as is written (Psalms 101: 6): 'My eyes are on the trusty men of the land, to have them at my side. He who follows the way of the blameless shall be in my service.' Aristotle said that whoever wants to hide the truth and whoever wants to hide a lie will become exhausted. Cato said that you may not promise something to one person and then also to another.

A text was found that described a very wealthy man, who spent all his money on charity. He went into the desert with a group of recluses to worship God there. One day, his friends asked him to go into the city (Jerusalem) to sell two donkeys that had gotten old and had become unfit to carry burdens. So, he entered the city and went to the marketplace. People would approach him, wanting to make a purchase and they would ask him if the donkeys were good, and he would reply: 'Do you think that, if they were good, we'd be selling them?' Others asked why the donkeys had hairless patches on their backs, to which he responded: 'Because they're old and lay down under their burdens, and we pull their tails and beat their backs, such that they have missing hair.' When he returned to his friends with both donkeys, he related to his friend all that had he'd done, and why he had not sold them. Then, they shouted at him and asked him: 'Why so bad?' 'Bad,' said the inept seller:

> This is because, believe it or not, I had left my home and deserted my heritage to seclude myself from deceitful lies – not to sell two old donkeys. Then, I had many donkeys, many camels, and cattle that I spent in worship of my Master [God] – How, then, can I now be untrue to my own faith by telling lies?

When they heard these words, they were afraid and feared him; they said no more.

106 | The Hebrew *Physiologus*

CHAPTER 25
ON LYING

'LIES' AND 'FALSEHOOD' are the opposite of 'the truth', as we learned from the researcher's saying that even the omission of the truth, when speaking, is done to defraud others. The vice of 'lying' also divides into several types: some (fictional) things are said that are not true while joking, telling tall tales, or in jest – things that never happened, and people also tell 'white lies' (that do not harm others) with good intentions or to escape personal harm. Nonetheless, it is best to avoid them ('white lies') as much as possible. There are those who lie to their friends or who swear falsely. Some, who are angry by nature, will always spew deceitful words; about them, Jeremiah the Prophet said (9: 4): 'They have trained their tongues to speak falsely.' And it is written (Leviticus 19: 12): 'You shall not swear falsely by my [God's] name, profaning the name of your God: I am the Lord;' indeed, it is like admitting that he (God forbid) no longer believes in Him. R. Yirmiya b. Abba said in 'tractate *Sanhedrin*' (*sic*, this reference should be to tractate *Sotah* 42a: 4): 'Four classes of people will not greet the Divine Presence: the cynics, flatterers, the liars, and the slanderers.'

In tractate *Ta'anit* (9b: 8), a story is recounted, that when R. 'Ulla arrived in Babylonia, he saw 'flying' clouds, so he announced there would be rain, but there was none. Then, he said, 'Just as the Babylonians are liars, so too, their rains are liars', since 'flying' clouds are a reliable sign of rain in the Land of Israel, but not in Babylonia.

The vice of 'lying' may be applied to a mole called *Topinara* by foreigners, that has no eyes and burrows underground. When it comes out into the open air of the world, it dies immediately. Thus, lies always move under some cover of the semblance of truth, for the sake of believability. Nevertheless, once light is shone on those (false) sayings and (deceitful) attempts, they die immediately, having been neutralised, recognised and known. As Solomon said (Proverbs 12: 19 and 22): 'Truthful speech abides forever, a lying tongue, but for a moment'; and: 'Lying speech is an abomination to the Lord.' God wants those who pray honestly, as did David, Solomon's father – that God remove deceitful ways from him, as stated in the *Torah* (Exodus 23: 7): 'Stay far away from falsehood.' Truthful people are in harmony in all of Creation.

In tractate *Sanhedrin* (97a: 6–7) it says:

> Concerning the lack of truth, Rava says: 'Initially, I would say that there is no honesty anywhere in the world. There was a certain one of the Sages, and R. Tavut is his name, and some say R. Tavyomei is his name, who was so honest that if they were to give him the entire world, he would not deviate from the truth in his statement.' He said to me: 'One time, I happened to come to a certain place, and Truth is its name, and its residents would not deviate from the truth in their statements, and no person from there would die prematurely. I married a woman from among them, and I had two sons from her.'

One day his wife was sitting and washing the hair on her head. Her neighbour came and knocked on the door. He thought, 'It is not proper conduct to tell the neighbour that his wife is bathing'. He said to her, 'She is not here'. Since he had deviated from the truth, his two sons died. The people residing in that place came before him and said, 'What is the meaning of this?' He said to them, 'This was the nature of the incident', and he told them what had happened. They said, 'Please leave our place and do not bring premature death upon our people'.

CHAPTER 26
ON BRAVERY

'BRAVERY' OR 'VALOUR', as researchers have written, has three aspects, it: 1) consists of physical strength and natural fortitude, which are not virtues; 2) is being fearless, strong hearted and always undaunted; and 3) is having the strength and courage to endure, with a brave heart, all incidents and tribulations that come to him. The latter two are true 'bravery'. This was explained in tractate *Avot* (4: 1 and in tractate *Tamid* 32a: 7): 'Who is mighty? He who subdues his [evil] inclination.' Also (Proverbs 16: 32): 'Better to be forbearing than mighty.' R. Ibn Gabirol wrote that it is appropriate to serve God in accordance with this virtue, like Moses and Pinḥas; and the well-educated should adopt this worthwhile virtue to avoid being called crazy, by behaving bravely along the good, straight path.

The virtue of 'bravery' may be seen in the lion, who always sleeps with open eyes and, if a hunter circles the area, the

Lion.
From chapter 26, 'On bravery'.

lion senses his presence and covers itself with its tail and hair, so the hunters will not see it. If the lion realises that there is no escape, it charges like a seasoned warrior, fighting fearlessly to the end.

We found that God is described as 'brave' (Psalms 24: 8): 'the Lord, mighty and valiant, the Lord, valiant in battle.' The Sun is also termed 'brave', as written (Psalms 19: 6): 'Like a hero, eager to run his course.' Also (Psalms 45: 4): 'Gird your sword upon your thigh, O hero.' In tractate *Yoma* (71a: 18), our sages quoted (Proverbs 8: 4): 'O men, I call to you', and R. Berechiah said: 'this refers to the *Torah* scholars, who are similar to women [physically weak] but are, nevertheless, mighty of mind [when engaged in *Torah* study].' Tullio said that he who wants to fight against scourges should arm himself patiently.

Once, in the Land of Israel, there was a big man, named Samson b. Manoaḥ, stronger than other men (Judges, Chapter 16) and he was discussed in tractate *Sotah* (9b: 23). R. Assi said: 'Tsor'ah and Eshta'ol were two large mountains that he [Samson] uprooted and ground one with the other'; and R. Shim'on said (10a: 5): 'The width between the shoulders of Samson was sixty cubits', as it is stated (Judges 16: 3): 'Samson grasped the doors of the town gate together ... He placed them on his shoulders.' One said that even the gates of Gaza weigh less than sixty cubits. And they said of Samson that he was created as an exemplar of this virtue 'bravery'.

CHAPTER 27

ON COWARDICE

'COWARDICE' or 'faint-heartedness' is contrary to 'bravery'. According to the researcher, there are three types: 1) for no particular reason, fearing for oneself, due to many imagined, still non-existent, troubles or evils supposedly coming one's way; 2) excessive fear of something real; and 3) being completely unable to withstand any sort of flaw at all. R. Ibn Gabirol wrote that this vice is found in lesser souls and prevents several good virtues, because it says: I won't deal with merchandise, so I won't lose money; I won't torture myself, so I don't get ill; I won't donate to charity, so I won't become poor; until this person finds excuses to do nothing. As written (Proverbs 22: 13): The lazy man says: 'There's a lion outside in the streets.' Indeed, regarding such a situation in which there is no salvation, one is justified in being afraid.

It was said about a man whom the king wanted to send somewhere dangerous, that he refused to go, so the king shamed him. That (cowardly) man said: 'I prefer being shamed by you and alive to being praised and dead.'

We can demonstrate the vice of 'cowardice' in the rabbit; there is no more faint-hearted creature than it. When it is in the forest, if it hears the sound of a leaf blowing in the wind, it will run away, flee from it.

Solomon said in this book of wisdom that nothing makes one more fearful than knowing the wickedness of one's deeds, because one fears punishment for them. Tullio said that the fear of death is worse than death itself, and that if you always want to live without fear, do good and only talk a little.

It is written that King Diogenes was the most cowardly of men and, due to his great fear and faint-heartedness, he was never calm nor quiet for even a single day of his life. But he had a loyal lover, who praised and glorified him, his situation and his status

Rabbits.
From chapter 27, 'On cowardice'.

all day long, who said that the king should thank God for all the goodness and advantages He had granted him. One day, the king summoned the lover and seated him on the royal throne, lit a big fire underneath it, and hung a sharp sword above his head on a thin flaxen string. The king commanded that a table be set before the lover with all sorts of sweets. Once the lover realised the danger, he began immediately to shout and beg the king to take him away from there. Then, the king said to him:

> In that case, never again praise my status and my life, for I am always in a more fearful and upsetting state than the one you could not withstand for a mere hour. For me, [the door into] Hell is forever open beneath me, and the sword of God's vengeance is [dangling] above my head, above the [yoke of] judgement hanging around my neck, and above the royal sceptre that one must wield to lead with great honesty.

CHAPTER 28
ON LARGESSE

'LARGESSE', also known as 'magnanimity', refers to thought, speech and action that is always beneficial, lofty and exalted, and getting happiness and pleasure from the provision of enjoyment and satisfaction to others. The researcher said one gets more pleasure when giving to others than when receiving from them, being optimistic, good-hearted and repaying good for evil and much for little.

This beautiful, spiritual virtue may be compared to the predatory bird *falconi* ('the falcon') that, even when it feels that it is starving to death, it will not eat meat from the carcass of an unclean creature and will prey only on large fowl. For it is said (Exodus 35: 22): 'everyone ... whose heart moved them', meaning in accordance with their 'magnanimity' that carried them to act in a certain way with 'largesse'. Solomon said (Proverbs 15: 15): 'Good-heartedness is a feast without end.' Alexander said that it is better to die than to be a vile ruler.

Roman books say that King Pyrrhus was an enemy of the Romans and one of his physicians wrote to the Romans that, for a certain sum of money, he would poison their enemy (Pyrrhus) and kill him. However, they replied that it would be wrong to do so, because their custom was to conquer by force, rather than engaging in malicious and deceitful tactics, at which time the Romans sent messengers with a message to King Pyrrhus that read: 'Beware your physician! For here is what he wrote to us.'

CHAPTER 29
ON VANITY

'VANITY', 'haughtiness' and 'self-glorification' are offshoots of the vice of 'pride', which has three aspects: 1) displaying one's personal wealth, wisdom and respect to receive more praise and respect from people and to make a name for oneself. As Solomon said (Ecclesiastes 7: 1): 'A good name is better than fragrant oil', meaning that, like fragrant oil, it should naturally advertise itself and its innate goodness, without seeking to reveal it. 2) Praising oneself, self-glorification, in the words of Solomon (Proverbs 27: 2): 'Let the mouth of another praise you, not yours, the lips of a stranger, not your own.' 3) Deceitfully displaying more than you are or what you are not, in order to receive (undeserved) praise and glory for it – and this is the vice of the hypocrites.

Peacock.
From chapter 29, 'On vanity'.

This may be compared to the peacock for the joyful and splendid sight of its colourful feathers, that it spreads out like a round fan, showing off its beauty, so all will say: 'What a stunning bird the peacock is!' David said (Psalms 10: 3): 'The wicked praises his own unbridled lusts', meaning that the wicked glorify themselves for want of praise. Solomon said (Proverbs 25: 14): 'Like clouds, wind – but no rain – is one who boasts of gifts not given.' Our sages said one should not covet grandeur and praise if one wishes to be good. Another added that after all the other passions have been conquered, this last one ('vanity') will still remain. Someone else said that, even for a single egg, a hen will raise her voice until the fox hears her. Tullio said, 'That type of prestige does not last long'. People must be judged by their deeds, not their words, since most people will take credit for things they did not do.

It is written in a book that a pious man was walking along and Elijah the Prophet came and joined him. As they were walking, they saw the carcass of a horse cast aside, that had an awfully strong stench, and so the pious man held his nose, while Elijah did absolutely nothing. They walked a bit farther and met a handsome young man with very curly hair. Then, Elijah held his nose. The pious man wondered about this and asked: 'Why, Sir, did you hold your nose before that handsome young man, but you didn't do it near that stinky carcass?' Elijah replied: 'My son, know that in God's eyes, that young man stank much worse, due to his vanity, than all the carcasses in the world.' As written (Psalms 101: 5): 'I cannot endure the haughty and proud man.'

CHAPTER 30
ON STRENGTH AND FORTITUDE

'STRENGTH' AND 'FORTITUDE' – often termed 'constancy' – refer to always standing firmly and being of one mind. This virtue depends heavily on faith, observance of the *Torah* (i.e., Jewish commandments) and having genuine opinions. But one must be wary of falling into arbitrariness or stubbornness, that do not take ethics into account, and beware of accepting mortal words of wisdom and counsel; for it is written (Proverbs 28: 14): 'he who hardens his heart falls into misfortune.'

Let us compare this virtue ('constancy') with the 'ever-singular bird' called the Phoenix, some call the 'sand-bird' in Hebrew. Job said (29: 18): 'I thought I would be as long-lived as the grains of sand', but he lived 315 years. When the Phoenix grows old and nears total exhaustion, it gathers well-dried branches from spice trees, makes itself a nest, gets in, turns its face towards the Sun, hovering with beating wings for a long time, until a fire alights in its nest, strengthened by the Sun before it. This bird is so strong in its commitment that, although it feels the burning flame, it does not leave the nest until it has been consumed; because it knows its inherent nature – that it is destined to be reborn. In the end, nine days later, out of the ashes remaining from its body, a tiny worm is born that lives and grows by natural energy, until, thirty days later, it becomes a bird, as it was originally, so that none other of its kind may be found like it in the world.

It is generally agreed (Numbers 23: 19) that, 'God is not man to be capricious, or mortal to change His mind'. As it is written (Psalms 89: 35): 'I will not violate my covenant or change what I have uttered.' The supreme holy ones (Jewish martyrs) had this virtue ('constancy'); those who endured trials and tribulations by fire and water, by sword and other deaths, with healthy hearts, as was stated in some of their eulogies. Especially in the *midrash* about Hannah and her seven sons (*cf.* tractate *Gittin* 57b; Book of the Maccabees 2) On this, David said (Psalms 57: 8): 'My heart is firm, O God; my heart is firm; I will sing, I will chant a hymn', meaning that David felt his heart was ready, strong and healthy; he will sing, because nothing can take him away from God. Tullio said that nothing is more proper for human beings than courage and knowledge. Cato stated that one should maintain one's opinion according to the nature of what exists. Another said that one should not praise he who starts, rather he who finishes. And another said that many started out to attain goodness, but only the strong and persistent attained it.

The Romans wrote that Lykourgos ordered and regulated religions and etiquette for his nation, but what he established was difficult to put into practice. To make people observe his regulations, that he considered to be just and necessary for the survival of the nation, he told them: 'I will go and pray to God that he will guide me in changing them as you wish. Meanwhile, swear to follow my rules, as they are, until my return.' And the entire nation swore to do so. Then, Lykourgos left their presence and never returned, so they obeyed his new codes of etiquette from then on. At the time of his death, he ordered that his body be cremated and that his ashes be spread in the ocean, so that, under no circumstance, would there be any opportunity for the people to bring his body into the city.

CHAPTER 31
ON FICKLENESS

THE VICE OF 'FICKLENESS' or 'inconstancy' – the opposite of 'constancy' – is when an individual's particular opinion or positions cannot be maintained for any length of time, indicating that his masters are evil and stupidity is frequently found in women.

This vice may be found in the sparrow, called *Rondini* by foreigners. Of all the birds, they mostly flit about, flying hither and thither, both in winter and summer, with no fixed location.

So, it is with the affirmations by the fickle. Similarly, it is said (Proverbs 14: 15): 'A simple man believes anything; but a cunning person accepts the plain truth.' And our sages said of the Egyptian Pharoah that he was inconstant – for example, when Judah told Joseph (Genesis 44: 18): 'you ... are the equal of Pharaoh', who makes decrees, but does not carry them out, makes promises, but does not keep them – but Joseph was, indeed, a man of his word.

Vulture.
From chapter 37, 'On drunkenness and gluttony'.

Similarly, our sages condemned Persian King Ahasuerus for being a fickle king (cf. The Scroll of Esther). Sallust said that 'fickleness' is a sign of stupidity. Aristotle said that the fickle person has no fixed opinion of his own.

In tractate *Sanhedrin* (107a: 2) it states:

> A person should never bring himself to undergo an ordeal, as David, King of Israel, asked to undergo an ordeal and failed. David said before God: 'Master of the Universe, for what reason does one say in prayer: God of Avraham, Isaac, and Jacob, and not: God of David?' The Lord replied: 'They have undergone ordeals before me, and you have not.' Then, David said: 'Examine me and subject me to an ordeal.'

Then (II Samuel 11: 2): 'David ... strolled on the roof of the royal palace and ... saw a woman bathing.' The sages said that Bathsheba was washing her hair, hidden behind a screen. Satan came and appeared to David as a bird. David shot an arrow at the bird, but the arrow pierced the screen, such that Bathsheba was exposed, and he saw her (II Samuel 11: 2–3): 'she was very beautiful. And the King [David] sent someone to make inquiries about the woman.' And it is written (Psalms 17: 3): 'Never will I speak of my depravity.' The sages interpreted David's words as: 'Would that my mouth had been muzzled and I'd have never spoken such words.' Indeed, we have been taught by this example that sins come to those who do not adhere to God's commandments or who fail when tested.

CHAPTER 32
ON TEMPERANCE

SUCH 'TEMPERANCE' or 'self-control' makes each man his own master, able to control his passions in one of two ways – first, by taking control of the cravings of the soul, which is true conquest; or, second, by stopping natural human will, arising from some sensory stimulation, for example, by food, sexual intercourse, pride, jealousy or anger and the like; if these urges can be stopped, it requires immense patience from the outset.

Let us compare this virtue of 'temperance' with the nature of the camel that naturally desires sexual intercourse more than any other living creature, because it follows the cow (female camel) for 100 miles just to have intercourse with her or see her. Nonetheless, the camel has control of its natural urges since, when it is in the company of its mother and sisters, it never touches them. It is also said of the camel that it is modest during sexual intercourse.

Solomon said (Proverbs 16: 32): 'Better ... to have self-control than to conquer a city.' And he said (Proverbs 16: 17): 'The path of the upright avoids evil; he who guards his soul protects his path.' In tractate *Berakhot* (7a: 22): And R. Yohanan said in the name of R. Yosei: 'A single *'mardut'* [regret in one's heart] is preferable to many lashes.' As stated in (Proverbs 17: 10): 'A rebuke works on an intelligent man, more than 100 blows on a fool.' And Rashi defines *'mardut'* ('regret') as being a self-imposed tyranny and heartfelt submission. Seneca said that no government is greater or lesser than self-government. Tullio said that if you want to conquer your passions, remove all superiority from yourself. Ptolemy said, fight your passions in your youth, because once you grow old, you will never leave them. Socrates said that it is harder to beat your passions than to beat the enemy, and whomever cannot control himself, certainly cannot beat others. Plato said that there are seven types of 'conquest' that he praises above

120 | The Hebrew Physiologus

Camels.
From chapter 32, 'On temperance'.

all: he who is modest and pure in his youth; he who is happy in old age; he who is generous while poor; he who fortifies himself with richness; he who is great but modest; he who withstands his troubles; and he who conquers his passions.

Thus, the Trojans wrote that their King Priam heard philosopher Corrado say that he who does not master himself is not human, so he wanted to test him. So King Priam found several individuals proficient in malicious gossip and self-aggrandisement, whom he sent to philosopher Corrado, to bad-mouth him and make him angry. The first one asked Corrado: 'To which family do you belong?' And Corrado replied: 'My lineage begins with me, while yours ends with you, because mine grows for me, while yours diminishes with you.' The second asked him: 'Are the clothes you're wearing beautiful?' He answered: 'A man is not known by his apparel.' And the third one said: 'Look here! Watch what this evil man will say.' And Corrado responded: 'He who states that your words are not lies – his statement is nullified.' The fourth said: 'Peace be with this fool.' His better replied: 'For years, you taught yourself how to gossip, while I taught myself to ignore it.' The fifth said: 'Go over there to that fool; but why would you speak with him?!' Corrado remained silent, not replying. Then, the king said to Corrado: 'Why don't you reply?' Corrado told him: 'My silence is a direct response to that type of question and such derogatory talk. It's more fitting that the ears reply than the tongue, because I can't keep bad-mouthing him as much as he's disgracing himself; while he's mastering my tongue, I'm still master of my ears.' Then, the sixth said: 'Your hair is curly.' To which he answered: 'Virtue depends on the heart.' The seventh said: 'My Lord, the King, beware Corrado, who says that I'm a gossip and a slanderer; and I saw him in the Greek camp.' Corrado responded: 'If that had been true, you'd have already stopped talking about it.' The eighth said: 'You're looking at a thief – that's how they talk.' Corrado answered: 'If you knew yourself, you wouldn't have said such a thing to me.' Then, the king, seeing Corrado's patience, called him over to sit beside him, and asked him how he was able to withstand such insults without getting angry. Corrado replied: 'Because I'm the master of their masters.' This means that Corrado has mastered God's higher virtues, while they are slaves of lowly, disgraceful vices. And there is no better way to anger the shameful than by silence, by making oneself seem intemperate about such things; because he who is angered by being denigrated to his face will only invite further debasement.

CHAPTER 33
ON LASCIVIOUSNESS

THOSE WHO cannot conquer their passions (who are lascivious and intemperate), stand in opposition to the virtue 'temperance' described above, and lasciviously and wantonly fulfil every obscene desire.

This vice is associated with the unicorn, a creature that primarily lusts after virgins. When it sees a virgin, it runs to her and naps in her arms, which is how the hunters can capture it.

Solomon said in the Book of Ecclesiastes (2: 3): 'I ventured to tempt my flesh with wine' and (2: 10) 'I withheld from my eyes nothing they asked for and denied myself no enjoyment.' However, he ended by stating that (2: 17) 'everything is futile and a pursuit of ill wind.' R. Yudan said in the name of R. Aivu (*Kohelet Rabbah* 1: 13): 'A person does not leave this world having achieved even half of his desire; rather, if he has one hundred, he wishes to turn them into two hundred.' Varro said that a lascivious person is not without many defects and wickedness. Seneca said that nothing lasts long enough for the intemperate. Socrates said that he who fulfils all his desires will end in disgrace and shame.

It was found written that there was a woman more modest and pious than the other women, who would not have intercourse with any man, but eventually, after a few women had spoken to her day after day about the great pleasure and joy intercourse provided, that she was swayed to try it. So, she summoned her lover, who had been asking for several days to lay with her, and they slept together a few times. Then, she began to think it was repulsive and an abomination – so she climbed up on the roof, fell off and died.

CHAPTER 34
ON HUMILITY

'HUMILITY' is the humbleness of spirit of someone who considers himself to be less of what he has in abundance, avoiding the median way. In *Avot* (4: 4), R. Levitas said: 'Be exceedingly humble of spirit.' R. Ibn Gabirol wrote that someone who has this virtue has already fortified his soul and prevented it from demanding the satisfaction of passions. A person must know that humility will earn that person respect. As we learned from II Kings (1: 13): 'a third [Arab] captain ... knelt before Elijah [the Prophet] and implored him, saying: "O, man of God, please have regard for my life and the lives of these fifty servants of yours!"'

We can compare the virtue of 'humility' to the sheep and the lamb, the humblest of creatures, that tolerate everything that happens to them, as written (Isaiah 53: 7): 'Like a sheep being led to the slaughter.' Therefore, the Children of Israel were also compared to sheep (Jeremiah 50: 17): 'Israel are scattered sheep' and the righteous and the pious.

David said (Psalms 37: 11): 'But the lowly shall inherit the land, and delight in abundant well-being.' And (Psalms 147: 6): 'The Lord gives courage to the lowly and brings the wicked down to the dust.' Solomon said (Proverbs 16: 18): 'Pride goes before ruination, arrogance before failure.' Also (Proverbs 22: 4): 'The effect of humility is fear of the Lord.' In tractate *Sanhedrin* (43b: 2), R. Yehoshu'a b. Levi also says:

> When the Temple is standing, if a person sacrifices a burnt-offering, he has the reward given for bringing a burnt-offering, and if he sacrifices a meal-offering, he has the reward given for bringing a meal-offering. But as for one whose spirit is humble – the verse ascribes him credit for his prayer as though he has sacrificed all the offerings.

124 | The Hebrew *Physiologus*

As it is written (Psalms 51: 19): 'True sacrifice to God is a contrite spirit.' Aristotle said that if you want to get to know someone, give him a government; the evil one will be proud and the good one will surrender. He also said that one should respect others, because respect is earned, not received. Longinus said that just as the birds lower and beat their wings to lift into flight, so must we lower and drive ourselves if we want to be uplifted. Socrates said that no matter how much respect you bestow on others, you'll never lose yours, because if one whom you honour does not compensate you with respect and honour, another will do so. And he also said that someone who wishes to be pleased should wear a gown of listening and humbleness. Briefly put, the fruits of humility are love and rest.

In Roman books, it is written that whenever they would send a military captain into battle, if he returned safely, victorious and with honours, they would do three honourable things and three disgraceful ones to him. The first honour was, that when he returned, the people would greet him outside the entrance to the city (Rome) in celebration, with great joy, rejoicing and songs of victory. The second honour was that they would mount him on a carriage pulled by four white horses and then the people would accompany him to the Campidoglio (the Capitoline Hill). And the third honour was that all the prisoners of war that he had captured in that war were tied behind his carriage. The first disgrace was that on that wagon they also placed a local despicable and worthless man, to thank the victorious captain and suggest that anyone could reach his stature if they mended their ways. The second disgrace was that the despicable man would slap him on the cheek several times and say: 'Don't take pride, because I'm a man just like you, and you're a man just like me, and maybe even I'll reach your stature.' And the third disgrace was that, on that day, everyone was allowed to shame him and remonstrate with him without fear of punishment.

CHAPTER 35
ON PRIDE

'PRIDE' IS THE VICE opposite to the virtue of 'humility', as stated by the researcher regarding the spectrum of vanity and the pursuit of power over others. And it exists in many forms, all of which do not recognise themselves and their delight in governing, and from which countless evils stem, among which are: denigrating superiors; ignoring the words of ministers and teachers; seeking revenge for every small thing; being an ingrate; and trespassing. In the end, proud people become loathsome, despised, sordid and hated by all God's creations. As R. Mari said (tractate *Bava Batra* 98a: 7): 'One who is haughty is not accepted even by the members of his household', as it is also stated (tractate *Sotah* 47b: 20, based on Habakkuk 2: 5): 'The haughty man abides not ... even in his abode.'

A comparison can be made between the vice of 'pride' and the clever *falconi* [some predatory avian species, though probably not actually a 'falcon' as we know it today], that always managed to rule the other birds. Once, there was a *falconi* so brazen that it overwhelmed an eagle, the king of the predatory fowl. Also, in the vicinity of its nest, it does not let any other predatory birds enter the surrounding area that it covets, where it rules, prevails and preys solely for its own benefit.

David said (Psalms 94: 2): 'Rise up, Judge of the Earth, give the arrogant their just desserts.' Solomon said (Proverbs 16: 19): 'Better to be humble and among the lowly than to share spoils with the proud.' And Job said (Job 20: 6–7): 'Though he grows as high as the sky, his head reaching the clouds, he perishes forever, like his dung; those who saw him will say: "Where is he?"' And it has been said (Proverbs 29: 23): 'A man's pride will humiliate him, but a humble man will obtain honour.' And R. Yohanan said in tractate *Sotah* (4b: 10): 'Any person who has arrogance within him is considered as if he were an idol worshipper', as it is written

126 | The Hebrew *Physiologus*

(Proverbs 16: 5): 'Everyone that is proud in heart is an abomination to the Lord,' and it is written (Deuteronomy 7: 26), concerning the destruction of idols: 'And you shall not bring an abomination into your house.' There have been many such reproachful sayings regarding this vice, until R. El'azar said (tractate *Sotah* 5a: 11): 'Concerning any person who has arrogance within him, his dust [i.e., his remains in his grave], will not stir [at the time of the resurrection of the dead]'; as it is stated in Isaiah 26: 19: 'O, let Your dead revive! Let corpses arise! Awake and sing for joy, you who dwell in the dust!' It has been said that there are three types who are unbearable: a proud poor man; a rich man in denial; and an old adulterer.

Plato said that pride corrupts people and that the prouder you become, the less aware of it you are. Another said that a person lacking humility should not have lovers. Yet another said that he wonders about proud people, who cannot abide living among human beings, nor with the birds and angels in the heavens, so they go down to the netherworld (Hell). Ben Sira said that, just as war diminishes the money, so pride may destroy the big palaces. Socrates said that it is not evil to coerce goodness, and nothing sustains love between people more than gratitude. And Solomon already told us (Proverbs 17: 13): 'Evil will never depart from the house of him who repays good with evil.' As such, one should let go of high spirits and mingle with people and repay their beneficence. As written in tractate *Avot* (3: 12), R. Yishma'el said: 'Be suppliant to a superior, submissive under compulsory service, and receive every man happily.'

R. Ibn Gabirol wrote in his book on moral qualities that one night, one of the kings had many guests, and all the workers and servants were doing his bidding. Then, the candle lighting his bedroom began to dim. He got up himself to fix it. The servants were frightened by this, saying: 'Why did you not command us to do this?' He replied: 'I arose as a king and sat back down as a king.'

CHAPTER 36
ON ABSTINENCE

'ABSTINENCE' is practised by someone who wishes to purify and protect himself from everything that is filthy and loathsome, to prevent the next such passionate desire.

This may be compared to the wild ass that refuses to drink water if it does not look clean and clear enough. And if it goes to the river and sees murky water, it will stand there for two or three days, not drinking until the water becomes cleaner.

Solomon said (Proverbs 20: 3): 'It is honourable for a man to desist from strife, but every fool becomes embroiled.' Also (Proverbs 20: 17): 'Bread gained by fraud may be tasty to a man, but later, his mouth will be filled with gravel.' In tractate 'Avodah Zarah, R. Pinḥas b. Ya'ir said: 'Torah study leads to caution.' Cleanliness leads to abstinence and abstinence leads to purity. Tractate

Ants.
From chapter 18, 'On diligence'.

Bava Batra (60b: 11) cites a *Baraita* ('an extracanonical oral tradition') from *Tosefta, Sota* (15: 11): 'When the [Jerusalem] Temple was destroyed a second time, there was an increase in the number of ascetics [*perushim*] among the Jews, whose practice was not to marry women, not to eat meat and not to drink wine.' A sage quoted Psalms (32: 9): 'Be not like a senseless horse or mule whose movement must be curbed by bit and bridle, to ward off what is close by'; indeed, men require seclusion. Aristotle said that the path of abstinence leads to all the virtues.

The ancients said that Alexander of Macedon was walking in the desert in Babylonia for a long time without any provisions because there was a great famine in the land and many of his people had starved to death. One of the hermits, who was with him, found a bee's honeycomb, which he brought to the king. Alexander took it and threw it into the river, saying: 'God forbid that I should live while all my people die!' However, many people jumped into the river to try and get some of that honey, and most of them drowned and died, because they were weak. Then, after a short walk, Alexander and his entourage arrived at their settlement and found everything they needed. So, he and his men ate and drank and were revived. Thus, for having suffered and curbed their energies, they lived, while the impetuous, seeking immediate gratification, died, their souls entrapped.

CHAPTER 37
ON DRUNKENNESS AND GLUTTONY

THE GLUTTON and the drunkard are known for eating and drinking in excess. The *Torah* had already spoken about this matter (Deuteronomy 21: 18) regarding 'a wayward and defiant son.' Our sages discussed these vices in tractate *Sanhedrin* (70a and 71a) and defined 'drunks' as those who drink more than half a *log* [an ancient liquid measure mentioned in the Hebrew Bible only once – a *hapax legomenon* found in Leviticus 14: 21] at one sitting, or not as part of a festive Jewish communal celebration; they thought this measure was equal to the weight of six raw eggs [about 600 ml/cm^3 or about 2.56 cups today]. Our sages also defined 'gluttons' as those who eat more than a *tarteymar* [an ancient Greek coin, weighing about 180 g] of meat at one sitting, or not as part of a festive Jewish communal celebration. The *Torah* says that one who wishes to be taught but does not find a teacher will likely end up stealing from people. From the drunk we move on to the one who wants to eat delicacies and the food of kings, even if only a little.

The vice of 'gluttony' may be seen in the vulture, that is so eager to eat a certain carrion, that it will go a hundred miles to have even one bite of that dead flesh. Therefore, it will always be found in war zones and the sight of vultures symbolises war.

'Gluttony' and 'drunkenness' destroy the memory, kill the intellect, make the blood murky, blind the eyes, weaken the strength, lead to prostitution, cause many bad ailments, reduce longevity, and deplete all goodness in a person. Solomon said (Proverbs 23: 20–1): 'Do not be of those who guzzle wine or glut themselves with meat; for guzzlers and gluttons will be impoverished.' Also (Hosea 4: 11): 'Lechery, wine and grape juice take control of the heart.' And (Proverbs 21: 17): 'He who loves wine and oil does not grow rich.' In the Holy Scriptures, mentions of wine always appear as descriptions of eating and drinking together. For example,

R. 'Ulla quoted a western proverb (in tractate Pesaḥim 114a: 3): 'One who eats a fat tail [alita] must hide in the attic [aliyata] from creditors who think he is wealthy. One who eats vegetables [kakuley] can lie down in the city's garbage [kikley] without fear of others.' And (Malachi 2: 3): 'I will strew dung upon your faces, the dung of your festal sacrifices.' R. Huna said (tractate Shabbat 151b: 5): 'those people who neglect the words of the Torah and turn all of their days into Festivals'; and R. Yehoshu'a said, 'Three days after death, the stomach of the dead bursts and an angel comes and throws it onto his face and says to him: "Take what you have wrought".'

Aristotle said that those who pursue food and drink are like beasts. Another said that a one can struggle in vain to conquer one's passions, but not succeed in conquering gluttony, because it is the reason for prostitution and pride and all the vices. Indeed, God's first commandment regarded fencing off (forbidding) a food (the proverbial 'apple' from the 'tree of wisdom' in Genesis 2: 17) from our first father, Adam, and mother Eve, and their failure to obey God's commandment brought death to them and their descendants, to the end of all the generations of Humanity. Some of our rabbis say that it was a grapevine, and others say a fig tree, but they all agree that one must be very careful about what one eats and drinks. As written (Proverbs 13: 25): 'A righteous person eats to satiation, but the belly of the wicked is never satisfied.'

CHAPTER 38
ON MODESTY

IN THE OPINION of researchers, 'modesty' is the virtue that insulates individuals from carnal desires (lust), whether it is a man married to a woman, or a married woman, that they be faithful to their spouses; even after losing a spouse, when they are permitted to seek a new partner, they should remain modest and decent.

Let us compare 'modesty' to the dove, that never fails in its trust and always maintains its alliance with its partner, and even after the partner dies, the remaining dove lives alone and lonely, not drinking clear water and not alighting on fresh, fertile trees. Solomon said (Proverbs 5: 18): 'Let your fountain be blessed; find joy in the wife of your youth'; and (Proverbs 6: 26): 'The last loaf of bread will go for a harlot.' And R. Yoḥanan said in tractate 'Eruvin (100b: 29):

> Even if the *Torah* had not been given, we would, nonetheless, have learned modesty from the cat, which covers its excrement, and that stealing is objectionable from the ant, which does not take grain from another ant, and about forbidden relations from the dove, which is faithful to its partner, and about proper relations from the rooster, that appeases the hen before mating with it.

R. Ḥiyya concurred, citing the biblical verse (Job 35: 11): 'Who gives us more knowledge than the beasts of the Earth, makes us wiser than the birds of the sky?'

An unusual tale appears in tractate *Shabbat* (53b: 20): 'There was an incident involving a man who married a one-armed woman, and he did not realise it until the day that she died, because she was so modest.'

Someone wrote that in order to be modest, one must avoid five things: 1) excessive eating and drinking, because it is impossible to stop physical urges at that point, like a fire spreading once it has been lit; 2) idleness, as a wise man said: 'Stop idleness and passion will cease'; 3) too much talking with women (mundane conversation, rather than *Torah* study), as stated (in tractate *Avot* 1: 5): 'Engage not in too much conversation with women'; 4) being in the company of jokers or those who promote lasciviousness; and 5) being in dens of iniquity, places rife with depraved behaviour or villainous talk, since a wise man said that passion is like a monkey, it wants to do everything it sees.

It is written, that in one city, there was a modest, chaste woman, who wanted nothing of the world's vanities. The minister of the city saw her and lusted after her, so he sent her several messages, inviting her to come and talk to him secretly; but he could not bend her to his will, until he decided to take her by force. So, he went to her home with heavy reinforcements and took her to his home. Once she realised that her cries and shouts would not be heard, she asked him to tell her what he saw in her that made him love her more than any other woman. He replied: 'Your dove-like eyes overwhelmed me.' Thus, she replied to him, after seeing how strong the love engendered by her eyes: 'I will do as you wish, but please allow me an hour to first prepare myself for you in a private room. Afterwards, I'll do your bidding.' So, the minister ordered that she be taken to a room. There, she shut the door behind her, took a knife and cut out both her eyes. Later, she opened the door and told him: 'Since you felt such enormous love for these eyes – I hand them to you, to do with as you please.' The minister was speechless and amazed, and sent her away, back to her home; she remained modest and chaste for the rest of her days.

CHAPTER 39
ON ADULTERY

THE VICE of 'adultery' is contrary to the virtue of 'modesty', and it is very bad when men have intercourse with unlawful women or have forbidden or indecent sex, that shortens human life. Physicians have said that one out of every thousand people dies due to mundane causes, and all the rest from coitus.

Let us compare this vice to European bats, called by foreigners *Barbastelle* – unique, nocturnal mammals, that are the most sexually depraved of all the creatures, dominated by lust, so much so that the natural order of things is not maintained, and males even mate with males, and females with females.

David said (Psalms 119: 150): 'When the lascivious approach, they are far from Your *Torah*.' This means that lasciviousness moves away from the teachings of the Hebrew Bible. Solomon said (Proverbs 7: 5 and 27): 'A strange, alien woman ... Her

Stoat (weasel).
From chapter 40, 'On integrity and good manners'.

134 | The Hebrew *Physiologus*

house is a pathway to Hell, leading down to Death's inner chambers.' And (Proverbs 29: 3): 'he who keeps company with harlots will lose his wealth.' Also (Proverbs 30: 15–16): 'Four never say: "Enough!": Hell; a barren womb; Earth that cannot get enough water; and fire ...'. David also said (Proverbs 30: 18–20): 'Three things are beyond me ... How an eagle makes its way through the sky; how a snake makes its way over a rock; how a ship makes its way over the high seas; how a man has his way with a maiden. Such is the way of an adulteress.' In tractate *Sotah* (3b: 11), R. Hisda said: 'Licentious behaviour in a home causes damage like a worm causes damage to sesame.' And (Deuteronomy 27: 15): 'Cursed be anyone who makes a sculpted or molten image.' However, R. Yehuda b. Nahmani argued in tractate *Sotah* (37b: 8) that: 'The entire passage of the blessings and curses is stated only in reference to an adulterer and adulteress.' In tractate *Yoma* (35b: 11), the sages (ironically) asked adulterers: 'Were you any more handsome than Joseph?', who was enslaved in Egypt but did not neglect his *Torah* despite his beauty and refused to commit adultery with his master Potifar's wife (Genesis 39: 1–12).

Seneca said that anyone who would consider the outcomes of fornication would abhor it from the start. Ovid said that you should not pay too much attention to the crying of women, because she may use it to trick you and can bat her eyelashes and shed tears on demand. Someone said (in jest) that if all adulterers were sentenced to be stoned to death, as dictated by biblical law, the stones could get it done, but not the executioners.

The Romans wrote that a baby boy was born to a king, who summoned his seers and his wise men to learn what would become of him. And they told him that if he saw the light of the world before the age of fourteen he would go blind. As such, the king commanded that they lock him up in a room in the tower, and there he stayed until the designated date, never having seen any living creatures or things besides the servants who brought him food and drink and met all his needs. On the aforementioned day, the king had him brought out and he was given into the care of the wise men, to teach him from books and the *Torah*, and to inform him that there is judgement and there is a judge (God), and there is a gentle Garden of Eden awaiting the righteous, where angels go up and down, and a Hell full of fire and brimstone awaiting the souls of sinners, where the wicked are led by the angels of punishment and devils to be punished. Then, they introduced him to all the creatures on Earth of all the species found nearby: men and women; sheep, cattle, horses and donkeys; dogs and cats; and birds and fish; reptiles and insects, and all the rest. And the boy asked them for each and every name, and they told him each one. But when he asked for the names of the women, someone answered him in jest: 'They are devils.' Later, the king asked his son what, of all those things he had seen, seemed the most appealing in his eyes. His son replied: 'What I found most appealing of all were the devils.' So, the king asked how he saw them. And his wise men told him what they had said to the youth, that there were female demons there. Then, the king said to his son: 'If so, my son, beware of them, lest they lead you to Hell.'

136 | The Hebrew *Physiologus*

CHAPTER 40
ON INTEGRITY AND GOOD MANNERS

'INTEGRITY,' 'good manners' and 'moderation' are virtues that make a person beloved both in Heaven and on Earth, and require the ability to find the median way in all actions, avoiding all extremes, very little and very much. This virtue is supported greatly by the attribute of embarrassment, being shamefaced and fearful of doing anything big or small that might not be dear to God's creations. That thought serves like a navigator steering a ship away from rocks and on its straight path. This is what Solomon said (Proverbs 4: 26–7): 'Survey the course you take, and all your ways will prosper. Do not swerve to the right or the left; keep your feet from evil.' As our sages have taught us in many words in all their essays, especially in tractate *Avot* and tractate *Derekh Erets* and in *midrashim* ('commentaries') about speaking, eating, drinking, even dressing and walking, and everything. In tractate Berakhot (8b: 13), R. 'Akiva said:

> In three aspects of their conduct, I like the Medes, and we should learn from their practices. When they cut meat, they cut it only on the table and not on their hands; when they kiss, either as a show of affection or honour, they kiss only the back of the hand and do not give the person being kissed an unpleasant feeling; and when they hold counsel, they only hold counsel in the field so others will not hear their secrets.

And tractate *Berakhot* also says (47a: 6): 'Two people who are eating from a single dish must wait for each other, but if there are three, each one eats when he wishes.' In tractate *Ketubot* [*sic*, this reference should be to tractate *Pesahim* 112a: 10], R. 'Akiva instructed: 'Do not enter your house suddenly.' And in tractate *Yoma* (4b: 11), R. Hanina said: 'A person should not say anything to another unless he calls him first', based on the biblical verse

Leviticus 1: 1: 'The Lord called to Moses and spoke to him.' And in tractate *Avot* (1: 5), R. Yosey b. Yoḥanan said: 'Let thy house be wide open, and let the poor be members of thy household.' Then, Joshua b. Peraḥiah said (1: 6): 'Judge all men with the scale weighted in their favour [giving the benefit of the doubt].' Also, Shim'on b. Gamliel stated (1: 17): 'I have found nothing better for a person than silence.' In addition, R. Hillel said later in tractate *Avot* (2: 6): 'In a place where there are no men, strive to be a man.' And R. Yosey added (2: 2): 'Let your friend's money be as precious to you as your own'.

We can compare this virtue to the stoat (weasel), also called an *Ermellino* by foreigners, the cleanest and purest creature in the world, with all white fur (in the winter), that eats only once a day, and no tainted meat passes its lips. During the rains, it remains in its burrow for fear of tainting itself with mud; it will not reside in a dirty place, unless it has been properly wiped clean. When hunters want to catch stoats, they make pits in the ground lined with clay or loam, and once the stoat leaves its location, they seal it, so that it cannot return there. Then, when it spots the hunters, it is so afraid that it runs back towards its former pit and seeing it sealed up, it surrenders to the hunters without getting dirty.

Solomon said (Proverbs 14: 8): 'It is the wisdom of a clever man to understand his course.' And (Proverbs 22: 5): 'Thorns and snares are in the path of the crooked; he who values his life will keep far away from them.' Our sages have said that anyone steeped in *Torah*, *Mishnah*, and in (rules of) good manners will not quickly become a sinner. As written (Ecclesiastes 4: 12): 'a three-fold cord is not readily broken.' Those that do not follow the *Torah*, the *Mishnah* and our rules of good manners are not part of our community. It was said in tractate *Berakhot* (32b: 11): 'Four things require bolstering: *Torah*, good deeds, prayer, and good manners.'

Andronicus (a Latin poet) said that everything has its measure, otherwise nothing could happen. Varro said that just

138 | The Hebrew *Physiologus*

as a horse behaves in his harness, so all the virtues behave with 'integrity' and 'good manners'. Seneca said: 'He who runs a lot will stumble a great deal.' And a wise man said that a small amount of bitter can blacken a large amount of honey. Plato said: 'Nothing can be wrong when everything is done right.' Avicenna said that he who wishes to always enjoy what he does, should not do those things too often. Solomon, in his wisdom said that the shame-faced will not be shamed, and the humble will not be conflicted, and the generous will not live in sorrow. When speech and regular actions are, first and foremost, practised with honesty and good manners, and become associated with someone, making that person amenable to brethren and even those far away – enough said. Solomon had many sayings (Proverbs 10: 11): 'The mouth of the righteous is a fountain of life, but lawlessness covers the mouth of the wicked'; (Proverbs 12: 14) 'A man gets his fill of good from the fruit of his speech'; (Proverbs 24: 26) 'Giving a straight-forward reply is like giving a kiss', etc. In tractate *Sanhedrin* (102a: 2), R. Abaye said: 'A covenant is made with the lips.' Now, lest we stray from our main topic, it is time to carefully restore order to our speech. In tractate *Pesahim* (113a: 3) R. Kahana said: 'It is better to turn over a carcass than to overturn your words [i.e., to break a promise].'

Albertus said that anyone interested in speaking intelligently should learn from the cock; before it even opens its beak to crow, it bats its wings three times. This teaches us three things about speech. First, if one is angry, do not speak in anger, because anger blindsides self-control, making the truth and the lies indistin-guishable, and impassioned speech is destructive; rather, stop and think what goodness and truth you really want to express. Second, determine with whom you wish to speak. Ptolemy said that before you speak, you must get to know the person you wish to address, because your words should be worthy of his value; if you are speaking to ministers or national advisers, you must prepare highly significant words of authority, loyalty, intelligence, and talk about chariots for warfare drawn by horses or other animals (e.g., tigers) or ostriches. With women, it is preferable to talk about happy things, desires, pearls of wisdom, various attire or household items. With the elderly, speak of the interesting; while with the pious, one should talk about things that are chaste and wise, and about acts of holiness. With the public masses, each artist should speak in accordance with his art. With peasants and villagers, speak about ploughing and reaping and everything associated with rural life. When speaking with fools, only when unavoidable, speak on their level. As Solomon said (Proverbs 26: 5): 'Answer a dullard in accordance with his folly.' With those who are sighing and distressed, speak words of comfort. And do so with each and every individual. And third, determine whether the subject to be discussed is suitable.

Afterwards, beware fifteen things: 1) excessive talk. As Solomon said (Proverbs 10: 19): 'Where there is much talking, there is no lack of transgression'; and (Proverbs 17: 28): 'Even a fool, if he keeps silent, is deemed wise; the intelligent seals his lips.' In *Mishah Pirkei Avot* (1: 17), R. Shim'on b. Gamliel said: 'whoever indulges in too many words brings about sin.' Socrates said: 'He who will not silence himself will be silenced by others.' 2) Fighting with others. As Solomon said (Proverbs 25: 8): 'Do not be quick to quarrel; consider the aftermath, when your friend puts you to shame.' Cato said: 'You should let yourself be bested by your friend's words, even if you could have beat him.' And our sages spoke of those (in tractate *Shabbat* 88b: 2): 'who hear their shame and do not respond.' 3) Saying contradictory things, such as David and his son Solomon, who was called *'leshon tahapukhot'* 'a treacherous tongue' (e.g., Proverbs 10: 31) and *'ish tahapukhot'* 'a shifty man' (e.g., Proverbs 16: 28). Cato said: 'Be contrary to others, but never to yourself.' Plato said: 'Foolishness is when a person contradicts himself.' 4) Speaking empty or foolish words of no consequence. 5) Being a hypocrite. Socrates said: 'Animals cannot be hypocrites, only humans can.' 6) Being a gossip and spreading slander. Our Holy Scriptures and our rabbis tell us that God punishes such bad behaviour. 7) Swearing false oaths

140 | The Hebrew *Physiologus*

(in God's name). Our sages said that the entire Earth shook when God gave the third Commandment (Exodus 20: 7): 'You shall not swear falsely by the name of the Lord, your God.' 8) Threatening or diminishing your friend. A wise man said that he who wishes another ill is considered an idiot, even if he isn't one. 9) Speaking harshly. Solomon said (Proverbs 15: 1): 'A gentle response allays wrath; a harsh word provokes anger'; and (Proverbs 25: 15): 'A gentle tongue can break bones.' Our sages praised gentle responses and calm speech with people. In the *Book of Ben Sira*, it is written that a lyre sounds good with a harp, but more pleasing is the sound of gentle speech. 10) Cursing your friend. The *Torah* says (Leviticus 19: 14): 'You shall not curse the deaf.' And Solomon said (Ecclesiastes 10: 20): 'Don't curse a king even in your mind.' When the sages asked R. Hanina how he had achieved longevity, he replied that he never went to bed cursing one of his fellowmen. 11) Using foul language. The Prophet Isaiah said (Isaiah 9: 16–17): 'And every mouth speaks impiety ... Yet, His anger has not turned back.' And our sages said that whoever uses foul language will have no place in the heavenly afterlife. Homer said that the tongue is the pen of the heart so, when the tongue is unclean, the heart is abhorrent. 12) Shaming and abusing your friend. In tractate *Kiddushin* (70b: 4), R. Yehudah says: 'Anyone who disqualifies others by stating that their lineage is flawed, that is a sign that he himself is of flawed lineage.' 13) Joking at the expense of others. Solomon said (Proverbs 17: 5): 'He who mocks the poor affronts his Maker.' Seneca said that one should not mock another, for no one is unblemished. 14) Speaking too seriously or by means of riddles. Solomon said (Proverbs 6: 12–14): 'A scoundrel ... lives by crooked speech, winking his eyes, shuffling his feet ... Duplicity in his heart; he plots evil.' Ben Sira said that he who speaks in riddles is trying to appear wiser than he really is. 15) Presenting yourself in a disorderly manner, in which there is no correlation between what you are saying and your facial expressions and body language.

A tale about R. Joshua b. Ḥananyah, who was referring to good manners, when he said the following ('Eruvin 53b):

In all my days, no person defeated me in a verbal encounter, except for a woman, a young girl, and a young boy. Who was this woman? One time, I was staying at a certain inn and the hostess prepared beans for me. On the first day, I ate them all. On the second day, I also left nothing on the plate. On the third day, she oversalted them, so as soon as I tasted them, I left them. She said to me: 'My rabbi, why aren't you eating?' I replied: 'I have already eaten something.' She responded: 'You shouldn't have eaten so much bread,' and added: 'My rabbi, perhaps this is because you did not leave a remainder on the first days? Didn't the Sages teach us that you need not leave a remainder in the pot, but [proper etiquette dictates] that you should leave a remainder on the plate?' [Derekh Erets Rabbah 6: 3]: 'We do not leave a small portion of the stew in the stew pot, but we should leave a small portion of the food on the plate.

What is the incident with the young girl? One time, I was walking along a path, and the path passed through a field, and I saw a young girl who asked me: 'My rabbi, isn't this a field?' [One should not walk through fields, so as not to damage the crops.] I replied: 'Isn't this a well-trodden path?' She retorted: 'Only because tramplers, like you, have trodden it.'

What is the incident with the young boy? One time, I was walking along a path, and I saw a young boy sitting at the cross-roads. I asked him: 'My son, which way goes to Lod?' He replied: 'This route is long and short, and that route is short and long.' I took the short-long path, and when I approached the city, I found that gardens and orchards surrounded it, so I turned back. I said to the boy: 'Didn't you say this path was the short one?' He replied: 'But didn't I also say it was long?' I kissed him on the head and said: 'Blessed are you, People of Israel, for you are all exceedingly wise, from your old to your young.'

INDEX

A

animal(s) 12, 23, 37, 58, 65, 139
    animal fables or parables 12, 37
Ant(s) 37, 90
Ass *see* Wild ass
Aurochs (extinct) 12, 93

B

Barbastelle see Bats
Basilisk (mythical) 12, 77
Bats 133
Baz see Falcon
Bear 12, 71
beast(s) 37
Beaver 12,
Bee(s) 13, 71, 89, 95
    Bee's honeycomb 128
bird(s) 13, 50, 58, 62, 74, 78, 100,
    102, 115, 118, 124–6, 135
    bird(s) of prey; predatory bird(s);
      carrion-eating birds 12–13,
      78, 102, 125
Boneh (Heb.) *see* Beaver
bull, wild *see* Aurochs

C

Caladrius (mythical) 12, 50
Camel(s) 105, 119

Castor see Beaver
cats 135
cattle 105, 135
chick(s) 62
Crane(s) 100
creature(s) 12–3, 36, 66, 68, 100,
    123, 134–5
Crow 58
    see also Raven

D

dog(s) 89, 135
Donkey(s) 79, 82, 105, 135
Dove 13
    Dove-like eyes 132

E

Eagle 12, 78, 134
    see also bird(s) of prey
Ermellino see Stoat

F

Falcon; *falconi* 12, 112, 125
    see also bird(s) of prey
fish(es) 23, 88, 135
fledgling(s) 74
fowl *see* bird(s)
Fox 13, 37, 89, 102, 114

144 | The Hebrew *Physiologus*

G
Grus see Crane(s)

H
hatchlings 66, 104
Hen 114
Hoglah (Heb.) *see* Partridge
Honeybee *see* Bee(s)
Horse(s) 114, 124, 128, 135, 138
horsewhip 84

I
insects 135

K
Karpadah (Heb.) *see* Toad

L
lamb 123
Lion 13, 77, 108, 110

M
Magpie 62
Mole 106
Mosquitoes 66
Mule 84, 128

N
Nesher (Heb.) *see* Eagle

O
Ostriches 139

P
Partridge 12, 104
Passerine(s) 74
Peacock 114
Peres (Heb.) *see* Vulture
Phoenix (mythical) 12, 115
Pirnitso see Partridge
Pola or *Pula see* Passerine(s)

R
Rabbit 110
Raven 66, 89
   see also Crow
reptiles 135
Rondini see Sparrow
Rospo see Toad

S
Sand-bird *see* Phoenix
Scorpion 89
Serpent (biblical) 36
Sheep 123, 135
sheepskin 103
Siren (mythical) 12, 88
snake(s) 98, 134
Sparrow 13, 117
Stoat 137

T
Tigers 139
Toad 12, 82
Topinara see Mole

U
Unicorn (mythical) 12, 122

V
Vulture 12, 129
   see also bird(s) of prey

W
Weasel *see* Stoat
wild beasts *see* beasts
wild bull *see* Aurochs
Wild ass 127
Wolf 86, 103
Worm 134